SPIRIT OF HAN

Text Contributions

LuYaw
&
Chi-Yun Chen
Abu Ridho
Eng-Lee Seok Chee
Rosemary E. Scott
Candace J. Lewis
Chen Huasha

Aileen Lau
Editor

Southeast Asian
Ceramic Society

SUNTREE

The Book

The Han Dynasty, often regarded with the Tang as a watershed period of Chinese cultural activity, value systems and socio-political structures, continues to fascinate scholars, anthropologists, historians, ceramicists and art enthusiasts the world over. The subject is constantly studied, discussed and up-dated, especially with on-going archaeological activity in China. Occasionally audiences are given the opportunity to view Han artefacts. The Spirit of Han exhibition is one such occasion and provides the opportune basis for this book.

In The Catalogue more than 200 colour plates illustrate the splendour of rare Han artefacts, providing interesting glimpses into the culture, artistry and practices of the time. The catalogue is fully classified and dated and the captions carry fine details to describe the five wares presented, that is, Plain Pottery, Painted Pottery, Glazed Pottery, Proto-Greenware and True Greenware.

Learned essays by leading ceramicists, scholars, and historians, namely, Lu Yaw, who provides the key-note article, Professor Chi-yun Chen, Abu Ridho, Eng-Lee Seok Chee, Rosemary Scott, Candace Lewis and Chen Huasha have lent considerable weight to the entire presentation. Their subjects are varied but related to the chronology and culture of tomb embellishments and the writers provide enlightening personal views of their acquaintance with and research on the Han.

It is hoped that this vivid study will bring fresh insight and much enjoyment to the reader, scholar and collector alike.

Editor

Co-published by The Southeast Asian Ceramic Society & Sun Tree Publishing Limited

Editor	: Aileen Lau
Editorial Production	: Sares Kanapathy
Design & Layout	: Sun Tree Publishing
Cover Illustration	: Eric Yeo
Catalogue Photography	: Lee Chee Kheong, National Museum, Singapore

Copyrights/Reprints
: © 1991
The Southeast Asian Ceramic Society
  Tanglin P. O. Box 317, Singapore 9124

Sun Tree Publishing Limited
Reprinted 1998

No part of this publication may be reproduced in any form without the permission in writing from the publishers.

ISBN No: 981 00 2961-6

Printed in Singapore by Chong Moh Offset Printing Pte Ltd

CONTENTS

4	Foreword
5	Preface
6	Acknowledgements
7	Map of China
8	The Dynasty
9	Rulers of the Imperial Han Dynasty
10	Providing for Life in the Other World
18	Han Dynasty China
26	Han Ceramics in Indonesia
30	Mingqi and Other Tomb Furnishings as a Reflection of Han Society and Culture
41	The Interchange of Motifs and the Development of Realism in the Decorative Arts of the Han
50	Tall Pottery Towers and their Archaeological Contexts
59	The Splendour of Han Pottery
71	*The Catalogue*
188	*List of Lenders*
189	Glossary

FOREWORD

The objects in the Spirit of Han exhibition are a testament to the high level of connoisseurship of Chinese rare arts among local collectors. Many are outstanding examples of the aesthetic and technological achievements of the Han dynasty. There can be little doubt that very discerning eyes searched and selected the objects in this exhibition.

But the eye is discerning only to the extent that it has been conditioned and trained to seek out and identify what are aesthetically excellent Han ceramic sculpture. Collecting, if it is to be successful, must be grounded upon solid and substantial scholarship of what is collected. The catalogue that accompanies this exhibition is testimony to the high level of scholarship that lies behind this exhibition.

Collection and scholarship on what is to be collected are however only two legs of a tripod of art appreciation. The third leg is an art market for connoisseurs to buy and sell rare art objects. This exhibition is the result of a growing rare art market responding to an increasing number of collectors who are entering the market better informed and aware of what they are collecting. If the art market continues to grow, then the future is bright for not only the rare art dealers and auctioneers, but more important, the Southeast Asian Ceramic Society and the National Museum.

The Southeast Asian Ceramic Society and its members, the rare art and antique dealers and the National Museum are willy-nilly parts of a system, interacting and dependent upon the others for their growth. Without the collector there will be no art market and fewer lenders to Museum exhibitions. But without the art market there will only be deprived collectors and a poor Museum. And without the Ceramic Society and the Museum there will be, fewer collectors to patronise the art auctions and dealers.

The National Museum is delighted to join the Southeast Asian Ceramic Society again (for the sixth time) in presenting this exhibition on Han ceramics. We would like to thank in particular Dr Kenson Kwok and especially Mrs Navaz Dastur for shouldering the major effort of organising this exhibition. For the Museum this exhibition is a time tested and proven way of increasing awareness of our cultural heritage through the appreciation of the rare arts.

The Museum is grateful to the Southeast Asian Ceramic Society for successfully persuading its members and friends to bring out items from their collections and therefore making this exhibition possible. The Museum hopes that this and other exhibitions may persuade some connoisseurs to consider placing parts of their collections on public display for longer periods of time.

The Museum joins the Ceramic Society in thanking all lenders to and sponsors of this exhibition.

Kwa Chong Guan
Director
National Museum, Singapore

PREFACE

Exhibitions of the Southeast Asian Ceramic Society have often reflected the changing collecting interests of our members. The Society's past exhibitions of celadons, of Vietnamese, and of Khmer ceramics, for example, have documented shifts in taste responding to the availability of certain pieces or wares to collectors in Singapore.

Large quantities of Han ceramics - sometimes of superb quality - have come on to the market in recent years. This has enabled us to mount what is, as far as we are aware, the most comprehensive exhibition of Han ceramics yet seen.

During the Han dynasty, ceramics were used for practical as well as ritualistic purposes. As the sub-title of this catalogue indicates, it is the ceramics made as tomb furnishings or minggi which are the subject of the exhibition. Only a very small number of the exhibits - such as the two eaves tile ends - can be identified conclusively as having been made for everyday life.

The exhibits are categorised by ware, and dated in accordance with current archaeological evidence. Many are models of structures, figures and household items. Although it is sometimes difficult to establish just how faithful these representations were, the objects still tell much about life in Han times, in a distinctive style that at its best is direct, humorous and earthy. The technical innovations of some of the wares - for example the multi-coloured lead glazed wares, precursors of Tang sancai - should also not be under-rated.

We are most grateful to Mr Kwa Chong Guan, Director of the National Museum Singapore, for his enthusiastic support of this exhibition as a joint project of the Museum and the Society, and have benefitted from the assistance of the Museum staff.

A venture such as this one is the fruit of the combined efforts of many people who freely volunteered their time to work at what were often extremely unsociable hours. Whether as Committee member, consultant or helping hand, each one has played a significant role in the mounting of the exhibition and the preparation of this catalogue. At the centre of it all, as convenor and overall co-ordinator, Mrs Navaz Dastur has been tireless in ferreting out, following up, and collecting together a formidable amount of material for the exhibition as well as the catalogue.

We owe the lenders to the exhibition a special debt of gratitude, for their willingness to lend and their patience with the documentation process. Pieces have also been borrowed from public collections, for which we would like to thank the National Museum Singapore, the Lee Kong Chian Art Museum, and the Raffles Country Club Art Museum.

Lastly, I would like to pay tribute to the Lee Foundation and the Shaw Foundation for their generous grants. These grants have enabled us to achieve a more professional standard of exhibition design, and to create more sophisticated educational media to illustrate the background and context of Han ceramics.

Dr Kenson Kwok
President
The Southeast Asian Ceramic Society

ACKNOWLEDGEMENTS

This exhibition and catalogue marks another chapter for the Southeast Asian Ceramic Society. Every quarter that we reached out to met us more than half way in helping the chief objective of the exhibition, which is to make aware the rich cultural heritage from the Han Dynasty. The co-operation of members, the overwhelming support of private collectors and dealers has made this exhibition possible and successful. As convenor for the exhibition, this has been a most enriching experience.

On behalf of the Organising Committee, I would like to thank the following:

- *Lau Wau Har, Mary Lee, Phang Lai Tee, and Nini Tiley for assistance with the translations and technical editing,*
- *June Buckingham for co-ordinating the exhibition video,*
- *Kwok Kian Chow for assistance with materials fo the video and catalogue,*
- *Suzanne Tory for the provenance of some of the illustrations,*
- *Rachel Gibson, Kristina Gardin and Millicent Yeo for assistance in documentation,*
- *Henri Chen, K. T. Goh, James and Poh Khoo, Amir and Marlies Mallal, Tan Hui Seng, and Frank Yip for supplementary exhibits,*
- *Earl Lu and John Pinnick for advice on financial matters.*

Navaz Dastur
Convenor

Organising Committee: Eng-Lee Seok Chee, Marjorie Chu, Kenson Kwok, LuYaw, Maura Rinaldi, Lise Young Lai

Southeast Asian Ceramic Society

Council Members
(1991)

Dr Kenson Kwok	President
Mrs Eng-Lee Seok Chee	Vice-President
Mr Steven Tan	Vice-President
Mrs Kristina Gardin	Honorary Secretary
Mrs Lise Young Lai	Honorary Treasurer
Dr Earl Lu	Council Member
Mr LuYaw	Council Member
Dr John Miksic	Council Member
Mrs Maura Rinaldi	Council Member
Mrs Navaz Dastur	Co-opted Member
Mrs Pamela Hickley	Co-opted Member
Mr John Pinnick	Co-opted Member

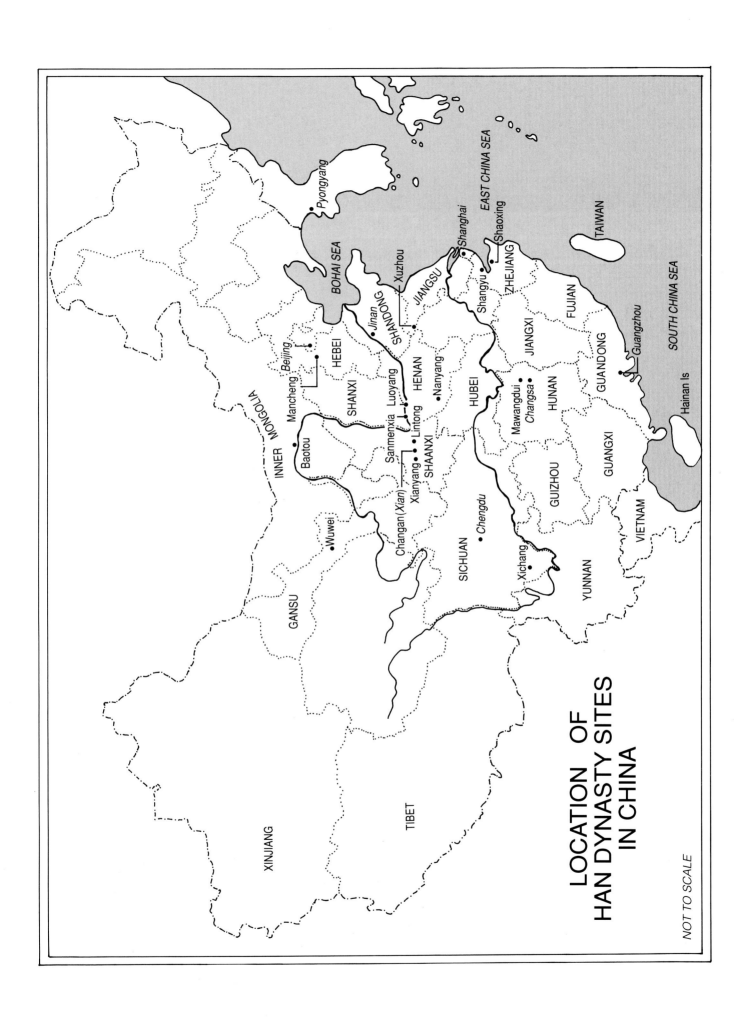

THE DYNASTY

WESTERN HAN .... 202 BC - AD 6

EASTERN HAN ..... AD 25 - AD 220

The Han Dynasty was the longest imperial dynasty in Chinese history. From 202 BC to AD 6, it was known as the Western (Former) Han, with its capital at Chang-an, near the present city of Xian.
It was interrupted by the reformer Wang Mang, who established the Xin (New) Dynasty, AD 9-23 and after this, the Han dynasty was restored. From AD 25 to 220 it was known as the Eastern (Later) Han, with its capital city at Luoyang.

RULERS OF THE IMPERIAL HAN DYNASTY

Western (Former) Han : Emperor Gao Zu   r. 206-195 BC
                                     Emperor Hui   r. 195-188
                                     Empress Gao Zu   r. 189-180
                                     Emperor Wen   r. 179-157
                                     Emperor Jing   r. 156-141
                                     Emperor Wu   r. 140-87
                                     Emperor Zhao   r. 86-74
                                     Emperor Xuan   r. 73-49
                                     Emperor Yuan   r. 49-33
                                     Emperor Cheng   r. 32-7
                                     Emperor Ai   r. 6 BC–AD 1
                                     Emperor Ping   r. AD 2–5
                                     Wang Mang as Acting Emperor   6-9
                                     Wang Mang's Xin Dynasty   9-23

Eastern (Later) Han :   Emperor Guang-wu   r. 25-27
                                     Emperor Ming   r. 58-75
                                     Emperor Zhang   r. 76-88
                                     Emperor He   r. 79-105
                                     Emperor Shang   r. 106
                                     Emperor An   r. 107-126
                                     Emperor Xun   r. 126-144
                                     Emperor Chong   r. 145
                                     Emperor Ji   r. 146
                                     Emperor Huan   r. 147-167
                                     Emperor Ling   r. 168-189
                                     Emperor Xian   r. 190-220
                                     Cao Cao as de facto ruler   196-220

The Wei dynasty founded by Cao Cao's son, Cao Pi, became one of the Three Kingdoms which divided China after the end of the Han dynasty.

Providing for Life in the Other World

Han Ceramics in the Light of Recent Archaeological Discoveries

by Lu Yaw

At Chinese funerals one may still see paper-made replicas of houses, cars, jewellery and money being burnt, a ritual performed in the belief that the dear departed may be kept supplied with needs and amenities in the other world. This practice has its origins in the remote past. In fact, it may be traced to the beginning of Chinese civilization in the Neolithic age when artistically crafted jade artefacts, sometimes in great quantities, were buried with the dead (Fig. A).

Burial items in those times were mainly actual objects used by the dead during their life time. Indeed slaves, entertainers, even their loved ones, used to be buried with the dead. (Fig. B).

Excavated in 1968, the twin tombs of Prince Liu Sheng and his concubine Dou Wan of early (second century BC) Han, the period with which much of this exhibition is concerned, were found to contain more than four thousand artefacts of one kind or another. It was a veritable treasure house resplendent with articles of precious and base metals, jade, lacquer, pottery, textiles, etc., most of which were clearly made for actual use. Some apparently had never actually been used as the lacquerware was found to be in mint condition; and would never have been accepted as Han Dynasty vintage if not witnessed as having been taken from the burial chambers of a known Han prince and his consort.

The now famous bronze oil lamp of a maiden holding a lantern bears an identification mark indicating its use in the palace of an earlier emperor, grandfather of the deceased prince (Fig. D).

Substitutes for slaves and other personnel who had served the dead began in the form of painted pottery, for example, of attendants and entertainers.

This practice of substituting 'proxies' developed progressively until late Han, when practically all supplies for tomb-furnishing were specially made for the purpose and predominantly in ceramics, except for some small items of personal effects, like personal seals, jade pendants and such like, closely associated with the departed in their lifetime; or other items which (were handy and) could conveniently be transported from the real world to the grave, like coins, which are found in abundance in ancient tombs. But even here clay replicas and tokens resembling gold money have been unearthed.

Substitution may at first have been prompted by humanitarian considerations, but was probably also motivated by economic factors. To sacrifice useful human resources and expensive horses and carriages must have been a very costly

Bronze lamp in the form of a maiden holding a lantern. (Wenwu). Chinese Relics Collection, Hebei Research Institute.

D

A grave site of the Liangzhu Culture (3000–2000BC). (Wenwu).

A

Remains and impressions of live horses and carriages buried in an 8th century BC tomb in Henan, excavated in 1956. (Kaogu).

business even for the ruling class. By the same token, articles made of the precious metals may have been a great drain on the resources of the mighty and affluent. Even copper, frequently featured in burial furniture in the form of bronze and brass was getting scarcer, on account of its use in minting money for the fast developing Han economy.

On the other hand the ceramic industry had grown apace. This plastic material, when in the hands of the skilled potter, was capable of being fashioned into endless forms for replicating an enormous range of subjects, living or inanimate. And as ceramic technology improved steadily during the Han period, its cost fell, and its quality and versatility increased, thus opening up a boundless scope for the creativity of the potter. From then on nothing was too expensive or impractical to accompany the dead, through the transit of burial, in their journey to the other world, for much was capable of being fashioned and replicated through the medium of ceramics.

Han society, under heavy influence of the Confucian teaching of filial piety, was much given to sumptuous tomb-furnishing. Even the not-so-affluent could do what they believed to be the right thing by their dear departed on a lavish scale but within their means. Hence the extensive finds in Han tombs today are predominantly in the form of ceramic ware.

Plain Pottery

A survey of Han ceramics is not complete without taking a look at the plain pottery of the time, that is, pottery unpainted and unglazed, at times decorated by just working on the raw material itself, as this forms the basis of Han ceramics. In fact pottery of this kind had been in existence several thousand years before Han. Even the cord-mark so common and conspicuous a feature among Neolithic and later pre-Han ages still lingers on in some of the Han pottery. This cord-mark treatment for the outer surface has the advantage of absorbing heat faster than a smooth surface, thus it was popular for cooking wares. This technical detail of plain pottery persisted in Han ceramic manufacture.

The basic material for making pottery at this or earlier times was refined clay with a high iron content. In its pure form it was used for making what we now call quality ware. When making artefacts for rougher use or for heating over the fire, sand was usually added. The latter form of pottery tends to be more porous though it can withstand heat better than the former, because of its sand content. The colour of pottery varies with the combustion condition in the kiln. Because of its iron content the fired pottery assumes shades of grey if, during the firing process, the atmosphere in the kiln is deficient in oxygen, a condition known as a reduction condition. The higher the iron content the darker the pottery — hence some pottery may even appear black. On the other hand, if the kiln atmosphere is rich in oxygen, that is, an oxidation condition, the fired pottery turns various shades of red.

Plain pottery was largely employed in making utility articles like drainage piping, building blocks and tiles, common kitchen utensils and the like. These are not much sought after by collectors, which may explain the relatively few exhibits of this type. As they were not protected by underground burial chambers, many have perished through the ravages of time. The roofing tile finials (Fig. 5,6) are perhaps the only examples we have of pottery wares for practical purposes.

The moulded grey pottery tiles depicting part of a procession (Fig. 11,12) were used to line the walls of the underground burial chambers. Likewise, the elaborately moulded hollow brick blocks (Fig. 7,8,9,10) were for framing the doors to such chambers. In early Han times grey pottery was also extensively used to replicate bronze ritual vessels.

Occasionally, common vessels (Fig. 4) used by the dead in their lifetime are found in tombs; these are mostly from tombs of the humble.

Two other varieties of this type of Han pottery deserve mention. One is the storage jar of a peculiar shape dubbed by the Chinese "cocoon" or "duck's-egg" jar (Fig. 2,3). This very dark pottery has a well-burnished surface, but on close examination traces of red or white pigment can sometimes be detected in the tiny recesses of the incised decoration on the surface. This type of pottery artefact, judging by its size and hardness, is likely to have been made originally for everyday use. When it was used for burial, painted decoration might have been added. And because the original surface was well burnished, the pigments were not able to withstand the ravages of burial. Cocoon jars found in early Han tombs are thought to date from the earlier Qin and late Warring States periods. They were confined to the present-day Shaanxi area.

Secondly, there is a later grey pottery ware, manifesting the same characteristics as the cocoon jar. Many such pieces are being found in Eastern Han tombs in the modern Sichuan area. Best known for their lively and humorously sculpted figures (Fig.13,14) they provide a glimpse into the life and activities of the Han people in the first and second centuries AD. Like the cocoon jars traces of pigment are sometimes found on the otherwise dark grey figures.

Painted Pottery

Unlike the painted pottery of Neolithic times, Han pottery was painted on biscuit already fired. This accounts for Han painted pottery often being denuded, at least partially, of its (otherwise) usually gorgeous pigments. For this reason painted pottery is said to have been made exclusively for burial purposes.

The body of this pottery may be grey or red. To paint the pottery the biscuit is first coated with a white slip. Only when it is dry colour pigments may be applied. Pigments used include black, red, white, aubergine, yellow, green and varying shades of these colours. The earliest works have only two or three colours, mainly black, white and red.

The important categories of painted pottery found in Western Han tombs are replicas of bronze ritual vessels (Fig. 28) and figures of attendants, entertainers, warriors, horses and carriages (Figs. 31—40). These are without doubt from tombs of people of consequence.

Since the 1950s several major tombs in this class have been excavated. The one found at Xingyang in Shaanxi province in 1956, a satellite tomb in an early Han imperial burial ground, yielded more than two thousand painted pottery statues of foot soldiers and mounted warriors, the grandest show of martial formation after the First Emperor's terracotta army of the preceding Qin dynasty. However, these figures are of a smaller scale, 60—70 cm high and details of the physique and dress are painted on instead of being sculpted as in the case of the life-sized Qin statues.

In another major archaeological discovery in 1988, in Xuzhou in the coastal province of Suzhou, warrior statues were found, as well as female figures, presumably court ladies, not unlike those illustrated in this catalogue (Figs. 31—33).

In 1990 a more unusual type of pottery was unearthed in Weicheng, another Shaanxi site in an imperial cemetery of early Western Han. They are different because they were found to be nude. But do not let us jump to the conclusion that Grecian sculpture had arrived in China at that early date. They were different in the sense that other than the head, which is modelled and painted realistically, and the anatomical badge to indicate sex — in this case they were all male — the trunk was a long cylinder with extensions like sticks to represent legs. They had no arms. From the neck down they were painted red. From shreds of decayed fabric found amidst them it may be inferred that these figures must have been clothed at the time of burial.

This assumption was confirmed in yet another major archaeological find in the later part of 1990, also in Shaanxi, at a site not far from present day Xian, famed as the capital site for nine dynasties. A kilnsite, rather than tombs, of vast proportions was found, comprising twenty odd kilns wholly devoted to producing pottery figures of the kind found in tombs of high ranking officials and imperial families.

Over a thousand nude pottery statues, both male and female, similar to those found in the imperial tomb as described earlier were discovered (Fig. C). In this case there was no indication of clothing as this was a factory mass-producing this kind of ware for the VIP dead. No doubt they would be clothed when the time came for them to join the retinue following their master on the journey to the other world; and presumably would be decked out according to their sex, station in life or position. Moulds for making them were also found as well as two whole kilns stacked with unfired ones, numbering a few thousand and standing on their heads!

There is reason to believe, as Chinese archaeologists do, that this kiln complex specialized in one production line, and was an example of officially-run industry, corresponding to imperial kilns in later ages like those found in Jingdezhen, whose function was to supply the needs of officialdom.

Perhaps more light can be thrown on the pottery at the exhibition if we take a look at the finds from another kiln, smaller in scope but more diversified in its products. This kiln was also found in the vicinity of Xian, from which painted pottery figures and domestic animals (Figs. 44—50) were unearthed. They have been linked to similar finds in early Han imperial family tombs.

Another archaeological discovery in 1989 that may be of interest is a burial site in present-day Sichuan province. It comprises a group of tombs appearing as if pigeon-holed into a cliff, a burial custom which found favour with ancient inhabitants of the remote south and south-west China, dating, in some cases, to 3,000 years ago. In this instance the tombs are dated to Eastern Han; some specimens of the finds are shown in Figs. 51—63.

Painted pottery also appears in the form of a wide range of utensils and containers copied, no doubt, from those for everyday use, some of which are in very interesting shapes, like the owl (Fig. 29,30) and the bear, favourite creatures much employed in Han art.

Cocoon jars are also featured in this category, but they are different from those dealt with in the Plain Pottery section in that they are usually smaller, and painted, indicating their function as part of the tomb furniture.

Not only are the shapes of painted pottery borrowed from bronze and lacquer ware, but the painted decorations were also derived from these other wares (Figs. 15—24), or from lacquered woodwork such as the elaborately painted coffins. These decorations commonly feature the cloud scroll, abstract concepts, geometrical patterns and the like.

A different kind of pottery, not seen in the north, has turned up in some quantity in the southern region, including Hongkong. It has a light beige colour, being rather high-fired (in the region of 1200°C).

It appears in a wide range of shapes, from utensils and containers for everyday use (Figs. 75—80) to models of stoves, houses and so forth, for burial purposes (Fig. 74).

These wares were coated with an inferior glaze, sometimes known as ash glaze, so thin and devoid of luster that it appears as a brown slip. In rather rare cases when applied in thick patches it drips downwards to form drops not unlike brownish olive-coloured glass. The glaze on the surface is often patchy.

C Nude figures from an early Han kilnsite near Xian. (Wenwu Weekly).

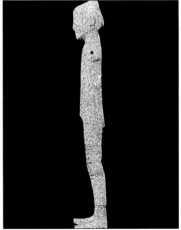

Glazed Pottery

This class of Han pottery is represented in force at the present exhibition. This is a reflection of the scale of its production, its variety and appeal to collectors. It also underscores the widespread practice of tomb-furnishing, extending from an elite class to a larger population.

To move from plain and painted pottery to lead-glazed pottery is undoubtedly a break-through in pottery making, even though it is only lead glaze, which cannot be of great practical value. But then this type of pottery was only extensively employed in manufacturing funerary artefacts.

Like the emergence of painted pottery, also mainly for burial purposes, glazed pottery did not replace plain pottery, but co-existed with it and even added variety to Han wares. However this type of pottery was not the first glazed ceramic ware to appear during this period; glazed terracotta or hard pottery, as the Chinese call it, was already in use. Proto-greenware (原始青瓷) or proto-porcelain (原始瓷), as termed by the Chinese, had been in existence more than a thousand years before Han, whereas the earliest lead-glazed pottery so far discovered has been found in tombs of the middle Western Han, in the second century BC. In other words, when pottery took a new form the older forms continued to co-exist with it for a long time.

Han lead-glazed pottery, however, was definitely a revolution in ceramic manufacture in that colour glaze was introduced for the first time. This was to develop into the famous **sancai** (three-colour) ware of the Tang period and beyond as **liuli** (琉璃) and **fahua** (法花) with more durable colour glazes in the Ming and the Qing.

In fact there are a few pieces (Figs. 101—106) in this exhibition which look surprisingly like **sancai** of Tang times. The large **hu** (Fig. 105) has an ochre glaze as base with green streaking all the way from the mouth rim down to the base; the small dish (Fig. 101) shows the play of two colours — dark green and salmon pink — creating a marbling effect. Upon close scrutiny this effect is observed to probably be the result of clever manipulation on the part of the potter, of the green glaze and the natural colour of the salmon-pink biscuit (as red pottery was most commonly used for lead-glazed wares). The technique employed was probably to coat the red pottery first with a transparent glaze, and before the latter completely dried, the green glaze was dabbed in such a manner as to create a marbling effect.

Other variations of this **sancai** effect can be seen in Fig. 99 and Fig. 100 where the green has streaked downwards from the mouthrim over the natural colour of the salmon-pink biscuit, and in Figs. 90—93 where the two colours shade and diffuse into each other in a subtle manner. In view of all this it would not be too far-fetched to dub this group of lead-glazed pottery "**Han sancai**". After all, is not Tang **sancai** lead-glazed pottery of a few colours? And the term "**sancai**" is applied to all Tang lead-glazed pottery whether it sports three colours or fewer — or more.

In Han lead-glazed pottery only shades of two colours, green and ochre, are evident; copper oxide produces the green colour and iron oxide the ochre, when the pottery is fired in an oxidation atmosphere, that is, if the air in the firing chamber has a rich charge of oxygen. The lead serves as a flux for the glaze to help it vitrify.

The illusion of another colour, a sort of silvery frost, is often observed on the surface of lead glaze, commonly on the green glaze. Until recently writers on Han ceramics, both in the East and the West, used to attribute this phenomenon variously to contact with mercury in different forms in the tomb, the precipitation of the lead in the glaze and so forth. Some years ago the Shanghai Silicate Institute conducted extensive tests and came to the conclusion that long immersion of the glaze in a moisture-laden condition allows water to enter the glaze and bring about

A rubbing showing two men playing chess and drinking, with ear-cups and a zun and ladle between them. (Pictorial Stones from Xuzhou)

Lu Yaw

its dissolution, causing the dissolved glaze material to ooze through the crackles in the glaze and deposit itself on the surface in a thin film. As the process continued layer upon layer of the deposits formed on the surface. When taken out from underground and seen in the light the hardened crusty surface gives the illusion of metallic lustre. Hence the two examples cited above take on the appearance of Tang three-colour ware. Pottery found in dry burial sites do not manifest this phenomenon.

As this kind of pottery was chiefly used for manufacturing funerary ware it was rather soft, maturing at 700—900°; even though fired at that temperature range the lead glaze had the tendency to run.

This group of Han pottery is seen in large numbers in the exhibition. The reason for this may be that it was then a novelty and, possibly, it could be produced with relative ease — thus cheaper compared to painted pottery. And, being glazed it has other advantages over the latter. To name but a few, it is clean to handle and can be kept clean easily, apart from having a sparkling appearance. No wonder its potential was fully exploited and all sorts of shapes were made of it to gratify all imaginable needs and amenities of the departed to ensure them a comfortable, even a luxurious, life in the other world. Consequently, in this group there are models of living creatures from human beings to domestic animals, and inanimate objects from kitchen utensils to towering structures.

However, lead-glazed pottery made a rather modest debut. The earliest examples found in mid-second century BC tombs in the interior regions of China are predominantly imitations of bronzes both for ritual and everyday use (Fig. 99, 107—113). The large **hu** (Fig. 99) and other containers like it, whose inside is unglazed, may have been in practical use for storage of dry foodstuff.

Obviously the granaries (Fig. 86, 87, etc) are scaled-down models of the actual pieces. So also are the **lian** (奁) or **zun** (樽), which might originally have been made of wood as the Chinese character for zun has the word representing wood for its radical, but only bronze ones have survived. They were used as containers for wine which was ladled out of them as depicted in banqueting scenes on stone or pottery slabs lining the burial chamber. (Fig. E).

As time went on models of other items were added. Well into the Eastern Han a heterogenous variety of artefacts of lead-glazed pottery emerged, catering to the needs not only of high society but also of the ordinary folk. This continued and culminated in stately watch towers, of which there are several in the exhibition. In the meantime, diversification of product seems to have accompanied the spread of this ware over a vast geographical area, east and southwards of metropolitan China, where lead-glazed pottery has been widely found.

There are examples in this exhibition where two lead glazes — green and ochre — are employed on the same piece either for colouring different parts of it (Fig. 92), or for one glazing over the other (Fig. 106). In the latter technique we may discern the harbinger of overglaze decoration of much later periods.

Proto-greenware/Proto-porcelain

Before proceeding further on Han ceramics, I feel there is need to make a digression.

Chinese ceramicists have classified all ceramics into pottery and porcelain, respectively called **tao** (陶) and **ci** (瓷). The basic distinction between the two lies in the raw material used to make the body and the temperature at which it is fired in the kiln. For **tao** common clay provides the raw material, whereas to make **ci** a special kind of clay — china clay or, more specifically, **kaolin** (高岭) — must be used.

As for firing temperature, the clay body of **tao** requires a temperature of between about 700°C to 1000°C to mature, depending on the material, beyond which it tends to lose shape and collapse; whereas a kaolin body needs a temperature of around 1300°C to become **ci**. A lower temperature will not turn **kaolin** into **ci**. This is why the white pottery of the Shang period, though having a **kaolin** body, is not **ci** because it is underfired. If glaze is used on **tao**, only a low-fired one like the lead-glaze will mature together with the clay body; and a high-fired glaze, like the felspathic one, is required to go with a **kaolin** body as lead glaze melts and evaporates at higher temperatures. On the other hand a felspathic glaze will not vitrify at a temperature suitable for **tao**.

*When these basic conditions are fulfilled the resulting product will not absorb water, or is almost non-absorbent, and will give a ringing sound when lightly tapped; and if all impurities in the **kaolin** are removed two more qualities can be attained: snow whiteness and near translucency. When porcelain first made its appearance in Europe in the fourteenth century or thereabouts it was already endowed with qualities of whiteness and translucency. But instead of using **ci**, a term used by the Chinese, the Europeans used the word "porcelain" for the Chinese **ci**. The Japanese, however, as they obtained the material from China embraced the Chinese nomenclature.*

*Many Westerners writing on Chinese ceramics, however, will not accept **ci** as porcelain, but variously refer to the Chinese **ci** as stone-ware, porcelaneous ware and so forth. The Chinese definitions for **tao** and **ci**, however, as stated above, are clear-cut, in my opinon.*

*I hope the reader will understand why this section is worded "Proto-greenware or Proto-porcelain", because greenware is the English translation of **qing-ci** (青瓷) — which, I believe, was first used in the West by Mary Tregear of Ashmolean Museum, Oxford — and **qing-ci** in Chinese means "green ci", or "green porcelain". Greenware was the first Chinese porcelain to dominate Chinese ceramic industry for centuries and was known in the Chinese context as "porcelain", during which time greenware was synonymous with porcelain.*

*But, what is greenware? To the Chinese it is **qing-ci** (so also to the Japanese, though they give the term a Japanese pronounciation "**seiji**"). Translated into English it is "green porcelain". But it should not be confused with the Han lead glaze pottery with a green colour, as the latter falls within the Chinese definition for pottery and the former the Chinese term for porcelain. It is also not "celadon" as tagged by the Europeans when they first came across this particular Chinese ceramic ware in the 14th or 15th century.*

Proto-greenware, however, is a term that has come into use in recent times, when Chinese ceramicists, through modern laboratory testing, have found something lacking in the greenware produced in the early days to qualify for the status of true greenware under the definition for porcelain — hence the name proto-greenware. If I may draw a rough parallel with another substance, proto-greenware (or proto-porcelain) is like crude oil and greenware or porcelain, petrol though, like the latter, greenware or porcelain also has different grades.

By the time of the Han, proto-greenware had been in use for about fifteen centuries, co-existing with all forms of pottery. It could never have evolved from pottery, as the basic materials used for making the one are different from the other as has been dealt with earlier on.

Examples of this type of ware are not many in the present exhibition. The few exhibits consist mostly of either large jars with relatively small mouths (Figs. 201—205), probably for everyday use and for storing liquids like wine, for which it has great advantage over pottery (being nearly non-porous), or of scaled-down models of ritual bronzes specifically for burial purposes. For the latter, however, pottery, especially of the lead-glazed variety, had the field to itself, as it was more attractive in appearance and cheaper to produce.

True Greenware

*It is thought that proto-greenware stagnated in its development since its debut in Shang (15th—11th century BC) times. Not only that, it has been known to suffer vicissitudes in its long history. The most notable decline must have occurred in the third century BC, for hardly any proto-greenware is found in burial sites of that period, which also coincided with the devastation of the Yue country (modern Zhejian and Jiangsu areas), where this type of ware was produced, during wars between the kingdoms of **Yue** (越) and **Cu** (楚). (A later greenware, the **Yue**-ware, was a direct descendant from proto-greenware.)*

Towards the end of the Warring States period (475—221BC), there was a revival of this ware as reflected in increasing quantities of proto-greenware unearthed in tombs dated from that period onwards. Even so, a lapse in quality occurred: often the ware had become coarser and more porous. Improvements became evident only when the Han dynasty was well advanced.

Recent archaeological evidence has revealed that among finds from tombs and kilnsites in the Zhejian and Jiangsu areas, datable to the end of Eastern Han, there is a type of ceramic ware with a thicker and more vitrified glaze and of a more truly olive-green hue than the usual proto-greenware; the body also assumes a lighter colour — varying shades of greyish-white — the result of a high titanium content in the **kaolin** clay which was abundant in this region of China. True greenware or porcelain as defined in Chinese (Fig. 210,211) commenced.

It has been pointed out before that the earliest proto-greenware so far discovered is from burial sites of about 13th century BC, that is, about fifteen centuries before true greenware was finally attained. This final break-through was achieved through a slow process of getting the raw materials refined to a higher and higher degree and, more importantly, of raising the firing temperature in the kiln. The former problem was relatively easier to solve; the latter depended on kiln construction.

Pre-Warring States kilns were built on flat land, sometimes half concealed in the ground — puny affairs of circular or oval form. Sometime in the Warring States period the body of the kiln was lengthened and built longitudinally on a sloping ground. By late Han both its length and the slope on which it was built had increased. With chimneys at the higher end this facilitates the draft in the kiln, drawing the flames and heat along the whole length of the kiln chamber, intensifying and retaining the heat inside for a longer period, thus raising the kiln temperature to an extent never attained before. In this way, barring the end-portion of the kiln chamber, the heat within the kiln could be raised to something like 1300°C, sufficient to mature a **kaolin** body into porcelain. This type of kiln is known as the dragon kiln and, with modifications over time, has been in use through the ages into the Qing period.

What then are the distinguishing features between the proto-greenware and the full-fledged greenware? In the first place, the body material of true greenware is more refined and of a greyish white colour, and harder, because it would have been fired at around 1300°C. The body material of proto-greenware, however, is usually darker, either grey or brownish, and contains a fair amount of impurities. Similarly, its glaze is not so smooth on account of impurities and usually shows a tinge of brown. In the case of the true greenware the glaze is smoother and more evenly spread, somewhat translucent and exhibiting a soothing green with just a touch of grey.

It deserves to be noted that from these kilnsites a proportion of the yields are black-glazed ware (Fig. 212); actually the black has a faintly green tinge, especially in the thinner parts of the glaze. The glaze material is not much different from that of the greenware glaze, except that the former has an iron oxide content of 4%—5%, whereas that for the latter only 1%—2%.

The blackware is usually found with a coarser and darker body than the greenware and is of a poorer finish. Apparently the black glaze was used to conceal these defects. Nonetheless it is another of the Han potter's innovations worthy of note.

(Figures in The Catalogue are referred to in this article.)

Acknowledgement

The author has drawn extensively from Chinese publications, which have emerged since the 1950s containing reliable and up-to-date material based on archaeological finds throughout China.

LUYAW

Curator, Lee Kong Chian Art Museum, National University of Singapore. Before this current position he was the Dean of Arts and the Deputy Vice-Chancellor of the Nanyang University in Singapore. His previous contributions for other Southeast Asian Ceramic Society publications in conjunction with exhibitions, have been numerous; namely, Chinese Blue And White Ceramics, (1978) and Chinese Celadons (1979). His major contribution was for Song Ceramics (1983) for which he wrote the descriptive text for the exhibits and the introduction.

Han Dynasty China

By Chi-yun Chen

During the four hundred-odd years of the Han, local cultures in different parts of China were re-moulded into an eclectic-syncretic high culture. Conscientious efforts were made to recover and re-examine the history and the cultural tradition of times long past. A multitude of ancient writings were recovered and re-edited into their present form; these included the "Six Canonical Classics", "Philosophic Works of the Various Schools", "Poetic Writings" and various "Technical Writings," which were classified and catalogued according to the Han Confucian scholastic scheme and interpreted with exegetic commentaries for the first time.

This historical-and-cultural-minded circumspection enabled the Han to syncretize the various ancient schools of philosophy into a grand Confucian synthesis. Syncretic Confucian ideology facilitated a reconciliation between the values of deep-rooted traditions and the exigencies of socio-political changes. This transformed the Han regime from a transitory reign into a lasting political establishment, which left behind a long-lasting cultural legacy. Long after the end of the Han dynasty, its tradition continued to mould the civilization of China, so much so that some ninety-five per cent of present-day Chinese (or the ancestors of practically all overseas Chinese) are still known as Han Chinese.

The Warring States, the Qin, and Early Western Han

Prior to the Han dynasty, China experienced several hundred years of civil war, leading to the formation of the seven powerful Warring States in 286 BC. During this period, Chinese culture made striking advances as evidenced by the widespread use of iron tools, prospering commerce and industry, the appearance of wealthy and influential merchants, private land ownership, liberation of serf-peasants, the development of big cities and extensive road systems, and heightened social mobility accomplished by the decline of **Feng-jian** (封建) nobility and rise of the new **Shi** (士) leaders. These new leaders included not only men of action (political reformers, diplomats, generals, merchants, and landlords) but also "men of ideas" who gave rise to the "Hundred Schools of Philosophy"– Confucianism (儒家), Daoism (道家), Yin-Yang and Five Elements Cosmologists (阴阳五行), Legalism (法家), etc. — heralding China's "Golden Age of Classic Thought" in 6th–3rd centuries BC[1].

These developments spurred the expansion of the contending Warring States into the frontier areas in the northeast (the Yen state's expansion into southern Manchuria), the northwest and the west (the Qin state expanding to the upper Yellow River bend and into the Ba (巴) and Shu (蜀) regions in present Sichuan), and the south (the Chu state incorporating the former domains of Wu and Yue (越) in present Jiangsu and Zhejiang Provinces, and the surviving Yue people spreading into the present Fujian and Guangdong Provinces).

Finally in 220 BC the state of Qin conquered the other Warring States and unified China. Under the guiding ideology of Legalism, the new imperial government initiated many drastic reforms. **Feng-jian** feudalism was abolished. The King of Qin adopted the new imperial title of Huang-di (皇帝) the August Emperor. The empire was divided into 36 (later 48) **Jun** (郡) Commanderies, sub-divided into more than a thousand Xian (县) Counties/Districts, and administered by centrally appointed officials. Extensive construction projects were undertaken. These included the great imperial capital, Xien-yang (near present Xian), highways from the capital to different parts of the empire, and the famous Great Wall. The mausoleum of the first Qin Emperor was a virtual underground palace and city complex, complete with defence fortress and artificial landscape. One section of this, first unearthed in 1974, covered an area of more than 12,000 square meters from which more than 7,000 life-size terracotta soldiers have been discovered.[2]

The imperial domain expanded into the frontier areas, for example, of the upper Yellow River (including the Ordos desert), and of areas in the far south in present-day Guangxi and Guangdong Province, and northern Vietnam. All these, except that in Vietnam, have remained permanent parts of China.

Advancement during this period included standardisation of scripts as well as of the measurement of weight, length, and volume, government-issued coins and the length of the axle of wagons in use throughout the empire. A most drastic attempt was made "to unify the people's thinking". In 213 BC, the Legalist Qin court ordered all books in private possession, except those of medicine, divination, and agriculture, to be confiscated and burned and those who engaged in private discussions of classical and historical works, or "used the past to criticize the present", to be publicly executed.

The Qin imperial regime was the shortest in Chinese history. It lasted only fifteen years and was overthrown in 206 BC by a popular revolution. In its wake arose the great Han dynasty.[3]

The Han dynasty had a modest beginning. Its founder, Liu Bang (Emperor Gao Zu), was from a peasant family. Many of his followers also came from a humble background. Liu Bang and his followers succeeded in defeating formidable rivals and rebuilt the empire. The early Han court faced many difficulties. The country had been recently wrecked by revolution and civil war. There emerged a strong reaction against imperial centralism founded on Legalism. Daoism, especially its teaching of "non-action quietism" (清静无为) became very popular.[4] Under the influence of Daoism, the early Han emperors and high officials conducted themselves with moderation, humility, and frugality.[5] It is recorded:

> "In all twenty-three years of his reign, Emperor Wen did not increase the size of the palaces or halls,...or vestments and carriages of the imperial household. He would not allow his favourite Lady Shen to wear gowns that trailed the ground. Nor would he have curtains with embroidered patterns on them... In constructing his tomb...he had pottery vessels used, not permitting gold, silver, copper, or tin to be used for ornamentation...for fear of burdening his subjects."[6]

The savings generated by such frugality enabled the court to make frequent reductions and exemptions of taxation on land.

The attitude of the early Han court was highly accommodating towards the border states and their peoples. In the south and the southeast, the Yue (越,粤) people were allowed to revive their autonomous kingdoms: Eastern Yue (东越), Min Yue (闽粤) and Southern Yue (南粤). Toward the nomadic Xiong-nu (匈奴) tribes on the northern frontiers, the early Han court adopted the conciliatory policy known as **he-qin** (和亲) "peace through marriage". In 198 BC, a chamber-maid of the emperor disguised as a princess carrying sizeable gifts from the Han court, was given to wed the Xiong-nu chieftain. This was repeated in 192, 174, 162, and 152 BC. The policy succeeded in preventing major military conflicts between the Han and the Xiong-nu for some seventy years.

Within the imperial domain, a compromise was effected between the centralized imperial system of the Qin and the decentralized **Feng-jian** system of the Zhou. The emperor was served by a court bureaucracy of appointed officials, i.e. the Prime Minister, the Grand Commandant, the Grandee Overseer, and the various ministries. The areas under the court's direct administration were governed by appointed officials at the Commandery and County levels. In other areas, the Han established a dozen or so powerful Principalities and more than a hundred Marquisates to help the court rule the vast empire. Some princely governments far outshone the imperial court in magnitude and splendour.

Under the influence of Daoism, the court seldom interfered with the affairs of the local communities. These were controlled by the strong and influential local figures, **Hao-jiang** (豪彊) magnates, who might have been remnants of **Feng-jian** nobility, leaders of large local clans, landlords, merchants, local government officials, or other local stalwarts. With the benefits of land tax reduction and exemption by the court, many local magnates later became big landlords or else came to be superseded as local leaders by the rising landlords.

The court policy of non-interference contributed much to the miraculous economic recovery in the first seventy years of the Han. It has been recorded that all households had sufficient provisions, while all the government storages were filled with copper coins and official granaries were overflowing, hence the rich of all classes, from commoner to high officials, marquises and princes, began to compete with one another in extravagant consumption and display of great wealth.[7] However, the strengthened Han court gradually tightened its control over the regional governments. In 179 BC, a Han diplomat persuaded the King of Southern Yue to become a Han vassal. Between 177–54 BC, attempts by the powerful princes to rebel were easily aborted. The invading Xiong-nu nomads were repelled and the Han began to support Chinese settlements along the northern frontiers.

Middle Western Han, 140–71 BC

While the early Han court favoured Daoism, Confucianism also developed vigorously on its own. As a reaction against the Qin proscription of scholarship, the Confucian devotion to book-learning and education received widening support and contributed greatly to the recovery of ancient literature, the most important corpus of which became the "Five Confucian Classics" — **Shi** (诗) Book of Poetry, **Shu** (书) Book of History, **Yi** (易) Book of Change, **Li** (礼) Book of Rites, and **Chun-qiu** (春秋) The Spring-and-Autumn Annals. Confucian scholars also gained much popularity in their criticism of the oppressive Qin regime and their advocacy of reform. The growing regard for the traditions and lessons of the past led to the writing of great histories, such as the **Shi-ji** (史记) (Historical Memoirs) by **Si-ma Qian** (司马迁) (145–85 BC), which became the model for Chinese "Standard Histories".

Under Emperor Wu, Confucianism replaced Daoism as the guiding ideology of the Han. In 136 BC, a number of official Erudites (博士) of the Five Confucian Classics were appointed by the court, leading to the formation of the Imperial University (太学) in 124 BC. Government schools were later established at the Commandery and County levels. Their students were assured of appointment to government posts after passing the graduation examination. Other channels of entrance to government services, such as recommendations or selections by high officials, also came under Confucian influence. Thus by the middle of the first century BC, nearly all important government positions were filled by the Confucian-educated, and as a result, members of this new official class are often known by the composite term "scholar-officials".

The court began vigorous centralization of the regional administration. Gradually, all regional princes and marquises were deprived of their power to govern; their fiefs came to be administered by officials appointed by the central government similar to the ordinary Commanderies and Counties. To further enhance centralized control, the empire was divided into 13 **Zhou** (州) Circuits (or Provinces), each supervised by an Inspector General **Ci-shi** (刺史) sent annually by the central government.

From 138 to 111 BC, the territory of the seceded Kingdoms of Dong-hai (in present Zhejiang), Min Yue (in present Fujian), and Southern Yue (in present Guangdong, Guangxi, and northern Vietnam) were reincorporated into the Han domain. In 108 BC, domestic troubles in northern Korea vanquished the Choson Kingdom, and as a result four Han Commanderies, including the famous Le-lang (near present-day Pyongyang), were established there. In the southwest, the Sichuan basin had long been part of the Qin state and was divided into the Commanderies of Ba (in eastern Sichuan) and Shu (near present-day Chengdu). In 135–114 BC seven new Han Commanderies were set up in the mountainous area in present western Sichuan, Guizhou, and Yunnan, which were populated by various scattered native communities collectively known as the "Southwestern Yi-peoples" (西南夷).

Toward the northern frontiers, the Han army battled the formidable Xiong-nu nomads for more than fifty years, from 129 to 72 BC. The drawn-out struggle split the Xiong-nu hordes into two: the less mobile Southern Xiong-nu surrendered to the Han; the more warlike Northern Xiong-nu began a long distance migration westward. Many historians believe, while some others doubt, that the migrating Xiong-nu reached eastern Europe some two or three hundred years later, where they were known as the Huns, who caused the fall of the Roman Empire. In 139–126 BC the Han diplomat Zhang Qian had sojourned in the northwestern frontiers and gained much knowledge of the area. In 115 BC, a chain of new Han Commanderies were established from the upper Yellow River bend to the famous outpost of Dunhuang (in northern Gansu). In 60 BC a Han Protector–general of Western Regions was installed to maintain security and order among some 36 statelets in the oases from present Xinjiang Province to the Soviet Kazakhstan.[8]

The Confucian ideal of social justice, together with the Han court's fiscal need, prompted Emperor Wu to adopt many drastic economic measures. Government monopolies of the production of iron and salt, the minting of copper coins, and the sale of liquor, as well as a Central Office for Price Control and Regional Office for Equitable Circulation of Goods were established. A new tax, highly discriminatory against the wealthy merchants, was imposed. These measures drove many merchants to join the ranks of officials for political protection or re-invest their wealth in land to become landlords, thus greatly strengthening the position of the officials and the landlords.[9]

Emperor Wu's measures against the local magnates were less effective. The court-appointed "harsh officials" executed or else ruined a number of powerful local magnates, usually heads of large clans or wealthy landlords. Such oppressive actions aroused great resentment from the rural communities and led to widespread unrest in the north China plain in 99 BC. The court was forced to nullify or relax its high-handed measures.[10]

Late Western Han and Wang Mang, 74 BC–AD 23

The country as a whole entered a long period of peace and prosperity. The ruling house slowly lost its initiative and rigour. Emperor Cheng was kind-hearted but ineffective, and entrusted his ruling power to maternal uncles, Wang Feng, Wang Yin, Wang Shang, and Wang Geng, who succeeded one another from 32 to 7 BC as Regent-of-state. Their nephew, Wang Mang, finally usurped the throne and founded his Xin dynasty in AD 9.

In the long run, the landlords, who had the stable financial resources to provide many years of Confucian classical education to their members, produced the largest number of scholar-officials. While some such scholar-officials tended to represent the interests of the local landed magnates, the majority of those in government service were honest and faithful in carrying out their duties. There were also a number of reform-minded ideologues who upheld the Confucian ideal that only a true sage was entitled to rule and to bring about "universal peace and equality"(**Tai-ping**) to the realm.

Emboldened by the victory of Confucianism but disappointed with the result of moderate reform, these ideologues began advocating more radical reforms by putting an end to the Han dynasty and installing a true sage on the throne. While Wang Mang came from a powerful family, he himself was a former student at the Imperial University and had the support of many Confucian ideologues who saw in him a sage-reformer. Under their influence, Wang Mang initiated many ambitious reforms aimed at founding a perfect state and society based on Confucian ideals. His measures included nationalizing landownership, limiting the size of individual holdings, distributing land to the landless, liberating slaves, abandoning the form of government which the Han had inherited from the evil Qin regime and establishing a court modelled after the virtuous Western Zhou as it was described in the Confucian Classic Zhou-li (周礼). However these measures proved ineffective and antagonized many conservative scholar-officials, landlords and local magnates, and former Han nobles. Together with the disastrous flooding of the Yellow River, Wang Mang's regime was brought to a tragic end in AD 23.[11]

Early Eastern Han, AD 25–88

The flooding of the Yellow River in northeastern China drove many peasants from their homes. These famine-stricken wanderers formed massive, roving armed bands, known as the Red-eyebrows (赤眉), who ravaged northern China. This gave the opportunity for the anti-Wang Mang uprising of the better-organized forces of the former Han nobles, Han loyalists, and the disaffected landlords and big clans. With the support of these latter groups, Liu Xiu, a member of the Han ruling clan and a former Confucian student of the Imperial University, prevailed over his rivals to become emperor (Guang-wu) of the restored Han dynasty.

The devastating flood and the political turmoil in northern China forced a southward migration. This initiated a long-lasting trend of southward migration of the Chinese population which contributed greatly to the cultural and economic development of southern China and some parts of Southeast Asia, a trend still ongoing in the 20th century. Following this trend, the restored dynasty moved its capital southeast to Luoyang, and was hence known as the Eastern Han.[12]

The early rulers of the Eastern Han refrained from any drastic political or economic measures that might antagonize the scholar-officials and the landed local magnates, but cautiously reorganized the court administration to consolidate their ruling power. Thus, while the imperial government's formal control over the realm became lax, the emperor's informal rein on the imperial government was tightened. This conservative policy succeeded in bringing back political stability to the imperium for the next sixty-odd years, sustaining a higher level of economic prosperity for more than a hundred years, and prolonged the Han dynasty for nearly two more centuries.[13]

After the fall of the Western Han and the failure of Wang Mang's reform, the official Confucian Modern Text School (今文) and Confucian reformism became suspect. The Eastern Han court continued to honour the Confucian Modern Text School as the state orthodoxy, which still produced, through its education and civil service system, a large number of scholar-officials to serve the imperial government. But many dedicated Confucians turned to the unofficial Ancient Text (古文) School for a pristine version of Confucian teaching aided by better textual criticism and scholastic exegeses; it was this unofficial Ancient Text School which outlived both the Han dynasty and the official Modern Text School to become the sole post-Han version of Confucianism.

Other high-minded Confucians were disillusioned with the ideal of "Grand Unity" or "Universal Peace", and turned their attention inwards to seek a lesser unity, peace in the self and its immediate surroundings, the family, the clan, and the local community, thus reviving the emphasis on filial piety, clan and kinship solidarity, and local community identity, which still characterizes Chinese cultural tradition to the present day.

Many Eastern Han Confucians refused to serve in the imperial government but lived in "retirement" in their native places, where they established and managed their estates, "nourished their spirit and cultivated their virtue", and found the material comfort, social prestige, local support, and popular influence derived therein much more gratifying than a career in the imperial government. They became leaders of the new local elite, superseding or transforming the less cultured landlords and local magnates, who, in order to compete with them, had to acquire a basic Confucian education and the necessary cultural trappings in emulation of this elite. This new elite establishment dominated much of the provincial areas and expanded its influence over the Eastern Han imperium through its connection with the scholar-officials serving in government posts. This development greatly enhanced the local autonomy, security, and economic well-being of the vast countryside, in spite of the weakness of the central government. This new elite establishment eventually outlasted the Han dynasty to become the **Shi** aristocracy in medieval China (3rd–9th centuries).

Middle Eastern Han, AD 89–189

The imperial court was reorganised by the early Eastern Han emperors who drastically reduced the power of the Prime Minister and other ranking Ministers, but greatly increased the importance of the **Shang-shu** (尚书) secretariat which was under the personal control of the Emperor. It also placed all staff of the emperor's palace-harem in the hands of the eunuchs. Palace politics and intrigues increased when a series of boy or infant emperors were chosen for the throne in AD 106, 107, 125, 145, 147, and 168 by powerful Regents who monopolized power at the court. These figurehead emperors, supported by the eunuchs, later assumed power and assassinated the Regents in a series of coups d'etat. Power struggles became rampant between the eunuchs as personal agents for the emperor and the high officials entrenched in the imperial government. This period also witnessed frequent invasions or uprisings by the frontier peoples as well as occasional local uprisings in the inner provinces.[14]

Indignant at court conditions, many Confucian scholar-officials voiced their strong moral strictures, known as **Qing-yi** or (清议) "Critical Discussion by the Pure Idealists", against government corruption. The **Dang-gu** (党锢) "Persecution of Partisans" launched by the eunuchs against their critics intensified the Confucian officials' protest movement, which gradually involved many discontented aristocrats, frustrated officials, idealistic literati, activist students, and ambitious local leaders. It developed from populist moral protest into widespread political resistance. The cooperation between the ruling house and officialdom, between the imperial government and local leaders, and the compromise between Confucian ideals and dynastic reality, which had long sustained the Han political, social, and cultural process, began to break down.

Late Eastern Han and the Incipient Age of Disunity, AD 190–265

Before describing the fall of the Han dynasty, it is necessary to discuss briefly the popular culture, and especially the evolving religious culture, which led to the Yellow Turban uprising wrecking the Eastern Han in AD 184.

At the beginning of the Western Han, pure philosophy and ideology were suspect. Daoism became popular because it was in some sense anti-philosophic and non-ideological. Confucianism later prevailed, owing to its realistic approach to learning, culture, and tradition as advocated by Xun-zi (fl.298–238 BC) and the early Han Confucians. The longing for spiritual enlightenment gave rise to an organismic cosmology, which viewed Heaven, Earth, and mankind as forming an organic whole, mutually affecting one another and following the same analogous Yin-Yang and Five Elements principles.[15]

The religious ethos at the imperial court was often embodied in the Yin-Yang and Five Elements mode of astronomical-astrological speculation and observance, in ritual calendars and almanacs regulating court ceremonies, and in the state cults of Heaven, Earth, and various gods. The same ethos may be found in analogous expressions in the religious practices of the general population. Folk cults and magic, long ignored and denigrated by the philosophers and literati of the late Warring States but which continued to be practised in the rural areas, received increasing support from the local magnates in Han times and subsequently the Confucianized new local elite. The mixture of Confucian precepts and cultic traditions brought about many apocryphal-prognostic **Qian-wei** (谶纬) works in late Western Han and early Eastern Han.[16] Archaeological finds, especially mural paintings in Han tombs, revealed well-developed notions of the after-life and the world beyond, which the Yin-Yang and Five Elements cosmology and the Confucian moral and historical teachings reinforced.[17]

In late Western Han, with the rise of Confucian advocacy of radical reform and the appearance of the apocryphal-prognostic works, a cryptic Celestial-Astrologist Almanac Embracing the Primal Origin Classic of Universal Peace and Equality (天官历苞元太平经) was compiled which preached a mystic change or purification of the dynasty.[18] In AD 141, a retired scholar-official Zhang Ling (ca. 34–156) initiated a Daoist religious community known as "The Way of the Five Bushels of Rice" (五斗米道) in Western China.[19] In about AD 165, when the Confucian movement was radicalized into political resistance, Zhang Jue and his two brothers began a popular Daoist religious movement, known as the Way of Universal Peace and Equality **Tai-ping dao** (太平道), based on the Classic of Universal Peace and Equality with Pure (Green?) Headings (太平清领书) The movement spread far and wide, receiving sympathy and support from the rich and poor, and gathering several hundred thousand followers. In AD 184, the movement culminated in an open uprising, with the insurgents using yellow turbans and flags signalling the death of the "Dark-blue Heaven" (the cosmic virtue of the Han dynasty) and the rise of the "Yellow Heaven" in accordance with the Yin-Yang and Five Elements cycles.[20]

The Yellow Turbans (黄中) were quickly suppressed by the joint forces of the frontier generals, the **Qing-yi** leaders, and the local elite, but the Han imperium was doomed. Leaders of **Qing-yi** and the local elite soon sent their armies against the eunuch-controlled court, and turned the last Eastern Han ruler into a mere figurehead. In the ensuing civil war, the Han realm was broken into three rival regimes, with the last Han Emperor Xian as a figurehead in the regime of Cao Cao, during the famous Jian-an (建安) era (196–220). This led to the division of China by the Three Kingdoms — Wei (House of Cao), Shu (蜀) (the surviving Han House of Liu), and Wu (吴) (House of Sun), AD 220–265, thus beginning the long Age of Disunity, 3rd–6th centuries.

The coalition of Confucian scholar-officials and the Confucianized local elite became a long-lasting **Shi** aristocratic gentry in the subsequent millennium. It contributed much to preserving the Han cultural tradition or even refining some parts of it (such as literature, art, philosophy, and religion) through the difficult times of civil war and barbarian invasion. After North China was conquered and ruled by the barbarians, the **Shi** gentry, with deep-rooted local community support and a tenacious hold on their cultural inheritance, were able to sustain an elemental cohesion in a divided China, even culturally assimilating their conquerors. The Han dynasty in producing the **Shi** gentry thus sowed the seed of its cultural continuity.[21]

Han Dynasty China in relation to South and Southeast Asia

The exact nature and extent of the cultural, people-to-people, contact between Han Dynasty China and Southeast Asia remains an open question.[22] Much depends on how one interprets some of the court records of Han time concerning the peoples who resided further south, southwest, or southeast of the southernmost Han Commanderies of Zhu-ya (珠厓), (Hainan island), Jiao-zhi (交趾) (now northern Vietnam), Jiu-zhen (九真) (now central Vietnam), and Ri-nan (日南) (now southeastern Vietnam). The most controversial piece of such records reads:

> "From the borders of Ri-nan, i.e. Xu-wen (徐闻) and He-pu (合浦) (both in the Lei-zhou (雷州) peninsula), going by boat for some five months, there is the state of Du-yuan (都元). Again going by boat for some four months, is the state of Yi-lu-mo (邑卢没). Again going by boat for some two months, is the state of Shen-li (谌离). Going on foot for over ten days, there is the state of Fu-gan-du-lu (夫甘都卢). Thence, going by boat for some two months, is the state of Huang-zhi (黄支), where the people's custom is generally similar to that of Zhu-ya.... It has many curious products, which have been presented to the Han court as tribute since the time of Emperor Wu.
> Previously, a Chief Interpreter belonging to the office of the Yellow Gate (of the Han Palace) together with those summoned by the government sailed to the sea to purchase pearls, beryl, curious stones and other precious things. They brought with them gold and silk.... the trading boats of the barbarians which carried them from one place to another also engaged in trade or raiding. It was a great danger to sail on these boats. The seas were rough and oftentimes they perished. It took those who did not quit the round trip several years to return to China. During the Yuan-shi period of Emperor Ping (AD 1–6), Wang Mang...sent envoys to the King of Huang-zhi with rich gifts and asked the latter to dispatch envoys to present live rhinoceroses to the court as tribute. It takes eight months to sail from Huang-zhi to Pi-zong (皮宗) and two months to the border of Xiang-lin (象林) in Ri-nan. South of Huang-zhi is a country called Yi-cheng-bu (已程不), where the Han Interpreter-envoys started their return trip."[23]

Scholars have tentatively identified Du-yuan to be on the northern coast of Sumatra, Yi-lu-mo as Arramaniya in southern Burma, Shen-li as Sillah near the Burmese city of Pagan, Fu-gan-du-lu as Pugandhara (Pagan), Pi-zong as Pulau Pisang (an island to the southwestern end of Malaysia), Huang-zhi as Kancipura (now Kanchipuram) in southeastern India, and Yi-cheng-bu to be in Ceylon.[24] Some have identified Shen-li to be on the east coast of the Malay peninsula, Fu-gan-du-lu on the west coast of the Malay peninsula, and Huang-zhi as near present-day Johor.[25] It thus seems that from about the middle of the 2nd century BC China had established some official trade and tribute-exchanging relationship with many local states in South and Southeast Asia. Since traditional China's official contact overseas usually lagged behind and followed earlier private, people-to-people contacts, it may be safe to infer that China's cultural and trade connections with the South and Southeast Asian native peoples can be traced to as early as the 4th–3rd centuries BC.

Although during the Eastern Han dynasty, especially in the 2nd century AD, the power and authority of China's imperial government was declining, Han records mentioned that occasional tribute-bearing missions still came to the Han court from the states of Shan (掸) (Burma) and Ye-diao (叶调) (Ceylon? Java-Sumatra?) as of AD 132, from Tian-zhu (天竺) (north India) in AD159 and AD160, and from Hai-xi Da-qin (海西大秦) (Rome or the Roman Orient) in AD166.[26] This indicates that, in spite of the shrinking of the Han empire's domain and its political influence abroad, continuous cultural and commercial connections were maintained by private individual Chinese with various local peoples in South and Southeast Asia, of which the official tribute-bearing missions merely served as ritualistic tokens. This pattern of China's overseas contacts lasted well into the 20th century.

Notes & Bibliography

1. See Cho-yun Hsü, Ancient China in Transition, Stanford University Press, 1965. Li Xueqin, Eastern Zhou and Qin Civilizations, tr. by K. C. Chang, Yale University Press, 1985.
2. For a popular, well-illustrated account, see Arthur Cotterell, The First Emperor of China, Penguin Books, 1981.
3. For general reference of the Qin and the Han dynasties, see The Cambridge History of China, vol. 1, Cambridge University Press, 1986.
4. For archaeological finds related to early Han Daoism, see Jan Yun-hua, "The Silk Manuscripts on Taoism", T'oung Pao 65 (1978), pp. 65–84.
5. Cf. Burton Watson tr., Records of the Grand Historian of China, Columbia University Press, 1961, Vol. 2, p. 79.
6. Cf. Homes H. Dubs tr., History of the Former Han Dynasty, Vol. 1, Waverly Press, 1938, pp. 272–275.
7. Han-shu (汉书) (Taipei: I-wen yin-shu kuan, Han-shu pu-chu edition) 24A and 24B, especially 24A:15.
8. Cf. Michael Loewe, Records of Han Administration, Cambridge University Press, 1967. A.F.P. Hulsewe, China in Central Asia: The Early Stage, 125 B.C.-A.D. 23, E. J. Brill, 1979.
9. Cf. Cho-yun Hsu, Han Agriculture, University of Washington Press, 1980. Chi-yun Chen, "Han Dynasty China: Economy, Society, and State Power", T'oung Pao 70 (1984), pp. 127–148.
10. See Huan Kuan (桓宽), Yen-tie lun (盐铁论), E.M. Gale tr., Discourses on Salt and Iron, E. J. Brill, 1931; Taipei: Ch'eng-wen Publishing Co. reprint, 1967.
11. Cf. Homes H. Dubs tr., History of the Former Han Dynasty, Vol 3, Waverly Press, 1955.
12. Cf. Hans Bielenstein, "Restoration of the Han Dynasty I – III", Bulletin of the Museum of Far Eastern Antiquity, 26 (1954), 31 (1959), 39 (1967).
13. For reference of this and the following discussion of the Eastern Han, see Chi-yun Chen, Hsün Yüeh (A.D. 148-209) : The Life and Reflections of an Early Medieval Confucian, Cambridge University Press, 1975.
14. R. de Crespigny, Northern Frontier: The Policies and Strategy of the Later Han Empire, Australian National University, Faculty of Asian Studies Monograph, NS. No.4, 1984.
15. Cf. Joseph Needham, Science and Civilization in China, Cambridge University Press, Vol. 2, 1969, p. 216 ff.
16. Cf. Tjan Tjoe Som, Po Hu T'ung, E.J. Brill, 1949, Vol. 1. Hans Bielenstein, "An Interpretation of the Portents in the Ts'ien Han-shu", Bulletin of the Museum of Far Eastern Antiquity 22 (1950), pp. 127–43.
17. Ying-shih Yü, "New Evidence on the Early Chinese Conception of Afterlife — A Review Article", Journal of Asian Studies 41:1 (1981), 81–85. Michael Loewe, Chinese Ideas of Life and Death, George Allen and Unwin, 1982. Martin J. Powers, "Hybrid Omens and Public Issues in Early Imperial China", Bulletin of the Museum of Far Eastern Antiquity 55 (1983), 1–55; also "Pictorial Art and Its Public in Early Imperial China", Art History 7:2 (1984), pp. 135–163.
18. Han-shu 11:5–6a and 75:31–33a.
19. Hou-Han shu (后汉书) (Taipei: I-wen yin shu-kuan, Hou Han-shu chi-chieh edition) 75:4.
20. Barbara Kandel, Taiping Jing, Hamburg, 1979. Chi-yun Chen, "Who were the Yellow Turbans? A Revisionist View", Cina 20 (Roma: ISMEO), pp. 57–68.
21. Chi-yun Chen, 1975, op. cit.
22. For further reference, see Wang Gungwu, "The Nanhai Trade: A Study of the Early History of Chinese Trade in the South China Sea," Journal of the Malayan Branch of the Royal Asiatic Society 31: 2 (June 1958), pp. 1-135. Ying-shih Yü, Trade and Expansion in Han China, University of California Press, 1967, pp. 172-187.
23. Han-shu 28B, tr. by Ying-shih Yü in ibid. pp. 172–173 (slightly modified by the present author), also Wang Gungwu, ibid., pp. 19–20
24. Ying-shih Yü, ibid., pp. 173, 176.
25. Wang Gungwu, op. cit., pp. 22–24
26. Ibid. pp. 24–30. Ying-shih Yü, Trade and Expansion, pp. 177–182.

Prof CHI-YUN CHEN (陈启云)

Born in Canton, China and now a citizen of the U.S.A. Has a Ph. D. from Harvard University and is a Professor of History with the University of California, Santa Barbara. Presently serving as a Visiting Professor with the National University of Singapore, he is the author of several books and also wrote a chapter on "Han Thought" for The Cambridge History of China, vol. – I, in 1986.

Han Dynasty Ceramics in Indonesia

by Abu Ridho

Edited by Mary Lee

The Jakarta National Museum has a pre-World War II collection of Han ceramics which once belonged to Egbert Willem van Orsay de Flines, a Dutchman. Mr Orsay de Flines bought many of the pieces in his collection from farmers working their fields, which means there is no detailed academic report verifying the source of the items. It is not clear when or how the Han ceramics arrived in Indonesia or who brought them there. Recorded history of Indonesia only began in AD 732 – some 500 years after the end of the Han Dynasty. It is quite possible that these items found were used by traders because Han ceramics were not export wares, and Indonesia at that time was a meeting place for merchants from the east and west.

Generally, farmers who say that these ceramics were discovered in their fields will only make an oral report, and even then, only of unusual items. The information they provide is usually very brief ("a mountainous area" or "a swamp"), consisting of the name of the village in which the find occurred, the name of the finder, the date of the find and how it occurred. While the farmers were once encouraged to hand over their finds to the government in return for a reward, many also sold them to dealers.

In March 1991, I met a villager from Curug, south of Cirebon, West Java, trying to sell a Han piece shaped like a stem bowl or wine cup (similar to one owned by the National Museum). He claimed he had found the bowl on his farmland. The dearth of Han ceramics reaching the National Museum in recent years suggests that either nothing has been found or else such finds have gone directly to private collections.

The pieces in Mr Orsay de Flines' collection are mostly low-fired earthenware, of brick red, grey or dark grey colour. The lead glaze colours include moss green, brownish red and muddy yellow. Some of the late Han pieces are made of a hard clay or proto-porcelain. Many of the pieces have moulded or applied reliefs of hunting scenes with riders, dogs, lions, dragons and pigs among rocky landscapes, as well as **taotie** masks.

The forms are rather limited, many shaped like bronze vessels, some very roughly made and some unevenly fired. Their condition too is varied – from good to bad; some pieces are badly damaged (Fig. 7) and others have lost their glaze (Fig. 8), presumably from having been too long in the ground.

Despite the absence of historical record or scientific data about Mr Orsay de Flines' collection, it is significant that in 1989 in Banten Girang (near Serang in West Java) a shard of a proto-porcelain vase of the Late Han period was excavated. The archaeological excavation was conducted by the Research Centre of Archaeology of Indonesia, led by Dr Hassan M Ambary. The solitary shard was found at a depth of 180 cm.

An interesting find much earlier was in the upper reaches of the Merangin River in the Kerinci area, in southwest Sumatra: a large bowl, 19.75 cm high with a diameter of 22.75 cm. It has square handles and three pillar-like feet. Made of grey-coloured earthenware without glaze, the Chinese characters on its base tell of Chu Yuan, the name of a Western Han administration in 48-32 BC. Mr Orsay de Flines wrote an article on this large bowl in Jaarboek KBG 1938 with a picture on page 180 of the magazine. A number of Han ceramics have reportedly been found in the vicinity of Kerinci.

Other finds of Han jars, ritual objects and other ceramics (see map) are reported to have been in Palembang, close to Jambi, Bengkulu and Lampung; Banten and Cirebon in west Java; Sambas in northwestern Kalimantan; Semarang in central Java and Baleko in south Sulawesi.

Some of the pieces from Mr Orsay de Flines' collection are illustrated and described on the following pages.

HAN CERAMICS IN INDONESIA

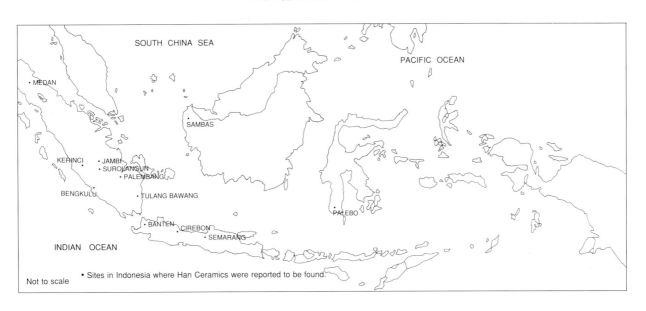

Hu with Cover
Mid-Han...........Brown, green and yellow-glazed earthenware
ht: 24.8 cm

The highly decorative glaze splashes are an unusual feature of this **hu**. The cover is dish-shaped. Reported to have been found in Kerinci, in the southern part of West Sumatra.

1

Hill Jar
Mid-Han..........Green-glazed earthenware
ht: 19cm, depth: 18.6 cm

Three paw feet support the cylindrical body of this vessel. The projecting lid carries the characteristic mountainous peaks or **boshan**. Spur marks are visible on the patterned square-sectioned rim of the lid.
Reported to have been found in Kerinci, in the southern part of West Sumatra.

2

Bowl with Handle (Yi)
Mid-Han..........Green-glazed earthenware
ht: 11.3 cm, length: 32.3 cm

The handle of this bowl is in the form of a dragon-head with an open mouth. There is a broad band of scored and punched geometric decoration on the side of the bowl, just below the rim. The green glaze has mostly degraded to a creamy colour.
Reported to have been found near Sungai Sambas, in the north of West Kalimantan.

3

Ridho

4

Grain Jar
Mid-Han..........Green-glazed earthenware
ht: 32.8 cm

Three sets of bowstring lines encircle this vessel which has a broad, rounded shoulder topped by a flat, moulded cover. There are three moulded feet. The glaze, which is of olive-green tone, has been chipped and abraded.
Reported to have been found near Tulangbawang, Lampung, Sumatra.

Hu
Eastern Han..........Green-glazed earthenware
ht: 37 cm

The glaze of rich moss green tone covers the exterior of this vessel, which has a broad moulded frieze on the shoulder, incorporating **taotie** masks and a hunting scene in a rocky landscape.
Reported to have been found in Surolangun, Sumatra.

5

6

Spoon
Eastern Han..........Green and yellow-glazed earthenware
length: 18 cm

Much of the glaze on the inside of the bowl of this spoon has flaked away, although traces of the yellowish glaze can still be seen. The rest of the spoon is green-glazed.
Reported to have been found near Cirebon, West Java.

7

Hu
Eastern Hu..........Green-glazed earthenware
ht: 31.1 cm

This heavily potted vessel has an orange-red body covered with a green glaze which has mostly degraded to a whitish-green colour. There are two moulded **taotie** masks with ring handles on the shoulder.
Reported to have been found in Bengkulu, Sumatra.

Hu
Eastern Han..........Green-glazed earthenware
ht: 39.3 cm

The **taotie** masks with ring handles on the shoulder of this **hu** are in unusually high relief. Much of the glaze has been abraded or flaked off. What remains has mostly degraded to a whitish colour, with small areas of green still visible.
Reported to have been found near Cirebon, West Java.

8

Bowl with Handle (Yi)
Eastern Han.........Ash-glazed earthenware
ht: 10 cm, dia: 18.5 cm

*The handle is horn-shaped. Areas of the glaze have flaked off.
Reported to have been found near Kerinci, in the southern part of West Sumatra.*

9

Stem Bowl
Eastern Han..........Proto-greenware
ht: 6 cm, dia: 10.8 cm

*The bowl, which sits on a slightly flaring, hollow foot, has a carinated profile.
Multiple grooved lines have been carved on the shallow slope of the shoulder.
The degraded green glaze shows signs of flaking.
Reported to have been found in Paleko, South Sulawesi.*

10

Further reading:

Abu Ridho: The World's Great Collections, Oriental Ceramics, Vol. 3 Museum Pusat, Jakarta, Kodansha Tokyo 1982 (2nd ed.).
Adhyatman, Sumarah: Keramik Kuno yan diketemukan di Indonesia, Yayasan Nusantara Jaya, Jakarta 1990 (2nd ed.).
Bambang Soemadio et al: Sejarah Nasional Indonesia jilid III, Balai Pustaka Jakarta 1975.
Flines, E.W. Van Orsay De: Korta Gida voor de Keramische Verzameling, Museum KBG Batavia 1949.
Groeneveldt, WP: Historical Notes on Indonesia & Malaya compiled from Chinese Sources, Bhratara Jakarta, 1950.
Hirth, Friedrich & WW Rockhill: Chau-ju Kua, Chu-fan Chi, St Petersburg 1911 (Photocopy Taiwan 1965).
Krom, B.J. Hindoe Javaansche Geschiedenis, Martinus Nijhoff, 'SGravenhage 1931.
Niojoe Lan: Tiongkok Sepanjang Abad, Balai Pustaka Jakarta 1954.
Poerbotijaroko, R Ng: Riwajat Indonesia I, Yayasan Pembangoenan Jakarta 1952.
Sellman, R.R.: An Outline Atlas of Eastern History, Edward Arnold Ltd, London 1954.
Wolters, O.W.: Early Indoesian Commerce, Cornell University Press, Ithaca-, New York 1967.
Yamin, Muhammad: Atlas Sejarah, Jambatan Jakarta 1955.

ABU RIDHO

Curator for the National Museum, Jakarta, Indonesia until his retirement in 1987. Author and Editor of several papers and books, in English and in Bahasa Indonesia, namely The World's Great Collections, "Oriental Ceramics", Vol. 3. Museum Pusat, Kondansha Series Tokyo, 1982, "Burmese Ceramics and White Kendis" in conjunction with Sumarah Adhyatman, 1985. Most recently he was associated with the exhibition and catalogue "Hizen Wares Abroad" The Kyushu Ceramic Museum, 1990.

He was a founder member of the Himpurnan Keramik Indonesia and is still a Council Member.

Mingqi and other Tomb Furnishings as Reflections of Han Culture and Society

by Eng-Lee Seok Chee

Separated from our era by a temporal distance of twenty centuries, Han culture and society are evoked through the agency of two primary legacies: the extensive literature of the period, which provides insight into the thought and ideas of the time; the other being the extensive tomb furnishings, which, taken together, offer fascinating glimpses of Han life.

Mingqi (明器) or sculptures produced expressly for burial, comprised an important category of Han grave goods. These "spirit articles" to console and comfort those who had passed into another existence encompassed an astonishingly wide range of objects. The clay **mingqi** figurines of people and animals, models of architectural forms and household utensils are a vivid graphic index to what was made, worn, consumed and used two thousand years ago. They can be profitably "read" by cross-reference with other grave goods like food remains and the personal possessions of the tomb owner. Painted and engraved scenes which enlivened many tombs form a rich lode of material that can be tapped for visual confirmation of the nature of prevailing mythological beliefs, as well as the social practices and technology described in Han texts.

Inventory slips (遣策) and tablets (赗方) discovered in some tombs provide an invaluable accounting of the grave goods buried there. They also clarify the terminology employed for different items during the Han period.

Tomb furnishings of the Western Han (206 BC-AD 9) differed markedly in range and content from those of the later, Eastern Han period (AD 25–220). However, far more dramatic differences can be seen in each period between the tombs of the priviledged classes and those of the poor.

At the apex of the social pyramid were the members of the court, officials and wealthy land-owners, who could afford to construct and equip grandoise tombs. In fact, a primary concern of each Han emperor when he ascended the throne was the building of his imperial mausoleum. For this purpose, a special department was set up and entrusted with the assemblage of suitably elaborate funerary articles.[1] Such mausoleums were many years in the making, and were largely realised through the forced labour of tens of thousands of prisoner-slaves These slaves of course, had no rights, only obligations to the State. However, in return for aiding in the building of the imperial mausoleum, the **Han Shi** (Han Histories) records that they were absolved from the death-penalty. Only a pathetic coin or two to send them off into the next world have been recovered from the tombs of prisoner-slaves, often buried with their shackles on in mass graves.

The graves of the **min** (民) or commoners, in Han times were also pitifully equipped. Tombs belonging to the **min** of the Eastern Han period, discovered in Luoyang, Henan, showed that impoverished commoners on the lowest level of the social pyramid could generally only afford a few coins and perhaps some roughly-made pottery vessels to serve as grave goods.[2] Thus, it is not from the spartan graves of the common people that we can learn much about Han life. For that, we have to turn to the well-furnished tombs of those who enjoyed a certain amount of wealth and power.

Tombs and Beliefs in the After-life

Early tombs of the Western Han period were conceived primarily as treasure chests.[3] The resting-places of the nobility, such as that of the consort of the Marquis of Dai at Mawangdui in Changsha, were shaft tombs sunk into the ground The centre compartment which housed the layers of coffins containing the body was surrounded by side compartments designed to hold luxurious burial items. Many of these items of bronze, lacquer, silk and jade were personal articles that had belonged to the deceased and been used in her lifetime.

By mid-Western Han, it had become the practice for tombs of the nobility to be dug horizontally into caves or hills. This allowed for the provision of chambers with more specialised functions. These tomb complexes were known as **dixia gongdian** (地下宮殿) or "underground palaces", which resembled to some extent, the main function rooms of official residences above ground. The tomb of Prince Jing at Mancheng, in Hebei Province featured side chambers for horses, and carriages and a capacious front hall to hold the important grave goods. However, perhaps the most impressive complex of the Western Han excavated to date is one found at Beidongshan, north of Xuzhou, in Jiangsu Province.

This ambitious structure, believed to be the resting place of a Prince of Chu, is composed of two sets of linked rooms: the main complex, which houses the burial chamber at one end, also has anterooms, two lavatories and a gallery; the auxilliary complex contains a total of eleven rooms. Their various functions are suggested by the built-in structures or grave items found there. Thus, weapons identify one room as an arsenal, pottery and lacquerware identify another as a store, while figurines of entertainers in a third area verify its use as a reception hall; the complex also boasts a kitchen and firewood store, an ice-cellar, a food store, a lavatory and a well.

The ordered layout of the "underground palace" at Beidongshan provides interesting clues to tomb culture in mid-Western Han. Here, the idea that the deceased should be well-provided for in the next world has been expanded upon. Besides the trappings of office and the personal possessions which had been accomodated in the vertical shaft tombs, lateral complexes like that at Beidongshan also attempted to surround the deceased with some of the practical comforts and sensuous pleasures that he had experienced on earth. To achieve this, both the public and the private aspects of court life were considered, and duly incorporated into the design.[4] Consequently, the primary complex which contained the coffin reflected the residential quarters of a Han palace, while the secondary complex represented the function rooms where banquets and entertainment took place, and the preparation of food carried out.

Underlying the highly elaborate procedures to build and secure a proper resting-place for the deceased, we can discern some of the assumptions held in Han times regarding the afterlife. It is clear that the continued existence of the **hun** (魂) or individual soul was a basic premise. The **hun**, which gives the living man his **qi** (氣) or spark of life was thought to journey to Heaven after death. It has been suggested that the famous T-shaped funerary banner found covering the coffin in Tomb 1 in Mawangdui chronicles this momentous journey of the soul. Divided into three sections, the banner depicts in ascending order, the underworld, the world of humans, and the heavenly world. The owner of the tomb is portrayed on this elaborately decorated silk banner, but coarser funerary banners of hemp or silk found in Wuwei, Gansu have only the name and homeplace of the tomb master inscribed on them, with perhaps the addition of simple sun and moon images.[5]

Despite the ambiguity of its message, the Mawangdui banner is tangible proof of a general conviction that strange mythological creatures inhabited both heavenly and lower regions. That these supernatural beings also appeared along the sides of the section representing the human realm suggested their unseen presence in the world of the living as well as that of the dead. Creatures with human faces and animal or bird-like bodies were an accepted if mysterious part of

the mythological pantheon, carved on tomb bricks and modelled as spirit articles of different materials. Male or female hybrids with scaly tails depicted in Han tomb art may have referred to the ancient legend of **Nuwa** (女媧) sister of the legendary emperor **Fuxi** (伏羲) who was reputed to have the body of a serpent and a human head. Another half-human creature is a gold-plated bronze man with wings and large elfin ears which was unearthed in Luoyang, Henan Province. This curious figure is believed to have represented a guide whose responsibility was to lead the spirit of the deceased to Heaven.[6] Twelve winged or feathered men also appeared on an elaborately contrived pottery lamp from Luoyang, designed to light up the tomb and protect it from the powers of darkness.[7]

The Rise of Mingqi

In the Han mind, the spirit world was a powerful one which had to be carefully propitiated by rites and rituals. From ancient times, the Emperor who served as the divinely-appointed intermediary for the country had to "scrupulously sacrifice to the upper and lower spirits"[8] and ensure the goodwill of the gods so that no disasters would befall his people. On the ordinary level, the patriarch who ruled the lives of his household would be the natural intermediary to intercede with the spirits on behalf of the family, after his own death and transformation into an ancestral being.

Filial piety has often been cited as a moving force which underlay the building and conscientious upkeep of tombs in the Han period. Certainly, the Confucian insistence on respect for elders was widely observed. The term **xiao** (孝) in its narrow sense referred to proper behaviour to one's parents; in a broader sense, it connoted a respect for seniority and duly constituted authority. Veneration for the old was promoted by official edicts and events in the Han court calendar. One of these was the annual observance referred to as "The Entertaining of the Aged."[9] To a gentleman of the period, carrying out the requisite sacrificial rites was considered to be "a part of the way of man."[10] Deprecating references to impoverished people who "have nothing to offer their ancestors at the seasonal sacrifices" can also be found in the writings of eminent Han historians like Sima Qian.[11] On funerary structures, numerous instructive examples of filial behaviour were depicted, the best known of these being the murals of the Wu Liang family shrines in Shandong Province.

Because the concept of filial piety encompassed obligations of the living to the dead, many households felt it necessary to show honour to the deceased by spending vast sums on tomb construction and furnishings. Grander tombs and more impressive arrays of grave goods became the trend by Eastern Han. Families strove to outdo each other in carrying out funerary rites which were surprisingly extravagant, in view of the unrest and pronounced economic difficulties which then prevailed. The State sought to dampen this rampant social rivalry by forbidding the burial of precious items of jade, bronze, gold and silver, and by regulating the numbers and types of grave goods that were permitted for each class of people in the society.

These developments led to a major change in the contents of tombs, as earthenware models or **mingqi** proliferated to take the place of the luxury items which had previously been employed as burial items. Many of these articles were deliberately fashioned to resemble the valuable articles they replaced. Pottery **hu** (壺) jars were moulded in the shapes of bronze models, and dipped in green, or less often, amber lead glazes to simulate bronze-like tones. The silvery iridescence that now decorates the surface of many Han pottery vessels through long burial belies their original darker "bronze" colouring.[12] Other pottery receptacles for cosmetics or food and wine attempted to replicate the appearance of the exclusive lacquerware designed for use in the homes of the wealthy. Borrowing the vermilion, green, ochre, white and black palette of lacquered articles, they emulate the elaborate scrolling designs and calligraphic line employed on contemporary lacquerwork. A painted **hu** (Fig. 22) and a painted cocoon jar (茧形壺) (Fig.15) in the exhibition are good illustrations of this practice. Being of little intrinsic worth themselves, these mass-produced clay tomb models which mimicked expensive bronze and lacquer were far less subjected to the looting and destructive attentions of grave robbers. As a consequence, they have survived in sufficient variety and relatively larger numbers to leave a composite picture of the people, animals, buildings and household articles of Han times.

Mingqi and Lifestyle

Increasingly, during Eastern Han, the tombs imitated dwellings. Civil and military officials, merchants and landowners built chambered tombs which echoed the layout of their manors, in the way that the princely tomb uncovered at Beidongshan replicated the original palatial residence above ground. Eastern Han tombs lined with bricks or stone slabs were often profusely decorated. In Sichuan Province, a number of tombs exhibit pictorial bricks (画像砖) with similar standardized designs. Showing a variety of topics, from banquets and lecture scenes to characteristic local activities such as taro digging and salt-making, these stamped and painted designs were mass-produced,[13] giving invaluable information on life in the southwestern section of the country. Some pictorial tomb murals from other areas must have been specially commissioned however, their subject-matter appears to be closely related to the life of the tomb-master.

A large brick tomb uncovered at Holingor in Inner Mongolia is a case in point. It has been painted with scenes that detailed the official career and achievements of the owner, who in life had been a military colonel. Vignettes showing the varied activities on his estate suggest that life on a prosperous manor, even in the outlying areas, was very similar to that near the heart of the empire. The cumulative impression provided by the tomb murals at Holingor is the self-sufficiency of the Han estate, achieved through the pragmatic diversification of productive activities[14] Many murals which show ploughing and tilling of the land or the reaping and harvesting of grain suggest that agriculture was the mainstay of the the estate. Depictions of the pasturing of sheep, oxen and horses indicate that animal husbandry constituted another important economic activity. Horses of course, were useful in many ways: they not only served as draught and transport animals, but their flesh also appeared on the table as food, with the exception of the liver, which was believed to be toxic. Because of their strength and swiftness, certain breeds of horses were highly prized. In particular, the fabled horses of Ferghana were regarded as status symbols among the gentry. The many examples of **mingqi** horses and ponies in the exhibition testify to the popularity of this animal as a subject of the Han potter. Horses were also cast in bronze to grace the tombs of the powerful, the most celebrated example being the bronze "flying horse" depicted with one hoof on a swallow, which was excavated in Wuwei, Gansu Province.

Other activities pictured in the Holingor murals which throw light on Han life are the scenes of workers picking mulberry leaves and dragging nets containing hemp through a pond. From the evidence of these tomb murals, it would appear that individual estates often planted their own groves of mulberry trees to feed silkworms reared for producing silk. **Ma** (麻) the hemp plant, was also cultivated, and commonly used for making rough cloth and rope. It was considered a grain in Han times, because edible cooking oil could be extracted from hemp seed. An inexpensive material, hemp was also utilised by the end of the Eastern Han period to make paper, a process invented at the beginning of the second century.

Food crops were processed to meet the immediate needs of the Han estate itself, and also marketed elsewhere to bring in revenue. Numerous milling sheds among the **mingqi** models have left a clear picture of the structure and operation of contemporary pounders and grinders, which were often housed together (Fig. 178, 179).

To produce the fermented beverages that played an important role in Han feasts, lower quality wheat, rice or millet grown on the estates were used. Two kinds of wines were brewed – **li** (醴) which could be made overnight, and **jiu** (酒) of superior quality, which required a longer and more complex process.[15] Vessels for wine were generally differentiated from food vessels. This is confirmed by the differing inscriptions on lacquerware wine and food dishes found in the Mawangdui tomb in Changsha. Only the very wealthy ate from fine sets of lacquered articles, which were even more costly than corresponding bronze ones. However, the pottery replicas of wine and food dishes made for tomb use suggest that those who could not afford lacquerware also employed separate forms of vessels for drinking and eating, made of humbler materials. The ovoid **erbei** (耳杯) or "earcups", with two winged appendages (Fig. 128, 129, 130) are pottery versions of a form of wine vessel common in the Han.

The self-contained economic and social unit that the Han estate represented was protected by a private militia. Tenant farmers owing allegiance to the master of the manor, who had to be prepared to take up weapons in his defense, comprised this readily-assembled defense force. Many of the clay architectural models recovered from Han tombs show farmer-soldiers armed with crossbows, on the alert for possible intruders. These archers are usually stationed at the corners of multi-storeyed buildings presumed to be watch-towers (Fig. 184, 185). Nevertheless, similar armed figures are also to be found at other types of buildings. On the upper level of an elaborate water pavilion (Fig. 187) can be counted a trio of archers standing with their cross-bows, in company with musicians, dancers and other figures. Below them, in the basin-like pond, are an equally motley assortment of animals.

A comparison with **mingqi** of later dynasties infers that few pottery models of furniture appeared in the Han. The absence of pottery chairs, a fairly common form of tomb ware during the Ming period, can be understood in the context of prevailing seating practices: in Han times, Chinese did not sit on chairs, but on mats like all Eastern and Middle Eastern peoples, many of whom still do so today. Low portable tables, placed close at hand, held dishes or other objects needed. Even a cursory survey of Han pottery

Upper Panel:
Hunting scene of men shooting birds with arrows
Lower Panel:
Harvesting and threshing grain on a Han estate
Tile Rubbing, Sichuan Provinces

figures shows many to be in a kneeling position. Apart from attendents who would be expected to assume this seemingly deferential pose, other figures, including musicians and chefs are also depicted resting on their haunches, legs hidden. Painted mural scenes in tombs confirm that many activities were conducted close to ground level, on mats and low platforms: holding discussions, playing **liubo** (六博), a dice game, listening to music, watching performances, or simply enjoying food and drink. Kneeling therefore was a natural posture, assumed before the introduction of chairs in China.

Tomb figures of wood and clay originally served as substitutes for live sacrificial victims. However, the barbaric custom of burying alive the retainers of the deceased gradually gave way to the more humane one of interring tomb effigies as companions for the next world. By the beginning of Eastern Han, a range of different earthenware figure types were placed in relevant sections of the chambered tombs, as reminders of the varied activities of life on earth. Besides the formal retinue of attendants and guards, the silent underground abode was also peopled by a lively assemblage of figures caught in naturalistic poses.

Among these, the figurines of entertainers must rank among the most engaging. From the evidence of pottery **mingqi** and tomb murals, it would seem that guests at more sedate banquets were treated to graceful performances of the **changxiu** (长袖) or long sleeve dance, accompanied by musicians playing reed or stringed instruments. On the other hand, exuberant exhibitions by drummers and acrobats added vibrancy to the **baixi** (百戏) or "hundred games" featured at festivities staged on a larger scale. One of the most beguiling of these events was the **qipan wu** (七盘舞) an acrobatic dance using seven overturned bowls, which required great nimbleness to leap from one bowl to the next without breaking them. As this popular Han dance was no longer performed by the Tang dynasty,[16] it is largely through the agency of tomb figurines and reliefs that a visual impression of the dance has been preserved for posterity.

An indispensable performer in the "hundred games" was the **paiyu** (俳優) or humorous entertainer. The most expressive examples of this comical character with the large head and bulging belly came from Eastern Han tombs in Sichuan Province. Acrobatic performers were often not of Han stock, but "imports" who came in along the Silk Route. The first foreign acrobats reportedly comprised official gifts presented by the King of Parthia to the Emperor Wudi in exchange for Chinese silk.[17] The alien origin of these entertainers who enlivened inumerable Han feasts can be deduced from their swarthy facial features, and their exotic hair and clothing styles. Sensitively captured facial expressions as well as subtle body movements characterise the best of these pottery figures. One that is able to elicit an empathic response from the viewer even after a span of two thousand years is the wonderfully doleful balladeer in the exhibition (Fig. 58). Though we are unable to hear his recitative, we can scarcely doubt that it is an infinitely sad tale.

In addition to acrobatic displays, Han accounts of New Year celebrations mention spectacular parades of

Jugglers and Dancers perform for Han gentry seated on mats
Tile Rubbing, Sichuan Province

mythological and auspicious animals. One of these creatures was the mysterious **hanli** (含利) which was reputed to "spit out gold."[18] More familiar to us is the animal imagery of a wall-relief uncovered in Yinan, Shandong Province, which shows a large dragon followed by a fish carried aloft by three men. Most likely pictured here is the **yulong manyer** (鱼龙曼延) or "fish-and-dragon procession," believed to have originated in the southwestern province of Sichuan. It has been remarked that these festive processions "are the ancestors of the New Year dragon parades which today still survive in Chinese overseas communities, including American Chinatowns."[19] The Yinan and similar friezes therefore, supply intriguing evidence that despite a major transposition in both time and space, some Han customs have persisted, with modifications, into the 20th century.

Mingqi and Food

Among Han grave goods, supplies of various foodstuffs were apt to take precedence, in the belief that providing sufficient sustenance for the next existence was a major priority. Well-furnished tombs of the nobility like Tomb No.1 at Mawangdui were generously stocked with both raw agricultural products and dishes of cooked food, prepared to the taste of the occupant. The primary grain foods of the Han, including rice, millet, wheat, barley, soybean and red lentil were all

At work in a large Eastern Han kitchen Tomb mural, Mixian, Henan Province (Wen Wu No. 10, 1972)

represented at Mawangdui, although the last two items were generally considered inferior substitutes consumed only by the very poor.

To hold grain, pottery urns echoing the form of actual granaries have been found in numerous tombs. Some of these urns are marked with the name of the grain they contained. Ceramic versions of the granaries fall into two main types. The first consists of models reproducing the main features of real Han granaries, namely, the roof, the tower which had both round and rectangular prototypes, rectangular openings on the side of the tower, and finally, an outside ladder-like stairway where the grain could be carried up or down. A stylized version, which was more functional to fill with grain offerings, eliminated the side openings in favour of a single circular roof opening. The outside staircase, being superfluous in this version, was also left out. Such stylized granary urns, generally raised on three feet in the shape of bears which connoted strength and virility (Fig. 86, 87, 114, etc), have thus become modified into basic storage vessels. Only their tiled roofs serve as tantalizing reminders of the original structure of Han granaries. Some pottery urns however, were conventionalized still further (Fig. 190), by being deprived of their roofs. Clues which remain to link them to their inspirational models are the typically attenuated shape of these vessels and occasionally, particles of grain discovered in their depths.

Snippets of information about Han cooking techniques as well as ingredients can be obtained by studying dishes of cooked foods preserved in the Mawangdui Tomb no.1 in conjunction with the 312 bamboo inventory slips found in the grave. From the inscriptions on the bamboo slips, we learn that the **geng** (羹) or stew, an important main dish was well represented. Listed were no less than nine **ding** (鼎) or cauldrons of **da-geng**, the unseasoned "grand stew" served as sacrifical offerings. The grand stews were pure meat dishes, unlike the ordinary, non-ceremonial mixed stews featuring combinations of meat with grain or vegetables.[20] Notable among the "ordinary" stews recorded on the *inventory slips are some unusual blends of ingredients, for example, "deer meat cooked with salt fish and bamboo shoots", and "dog meat cooked with sonchus," a type of wild grass.*

*Twentieth century curiosity about Han cooking methods can be partly assuaged by looking at the numerous pottery models of stoves and kitchen utensils recovered from tombs. In common with pottery granaries, stoves and cooking ranges were among the first **mingqi** to appear, and widely found in tombs of latter Western Han[21]. Undoubtedly, the close linkage of the range with the preparation of sustenance for the next world was responsible for its inclusion even in imperial tombs.[22] Two main versions of the pottery stove were made, one being rectangular, the other rounded at one end like a horseshoe. Cooking holes are set into the upper surface, on which one or more pots may be modelled (Fig. 140, 141). Indicated in relief around the cooking holes are kitchen utensils, or images of fish or other food (Fig. 142). A chimney raised at one end of the range is occasionally included, but the opening to the fire-chamber appears to be a standard feature. Actual ranges would have varied in size depending on the status or composition of the household, and large ones may have required a kitchen apprentice to bring fuel and stoke the flames. A humble attendent, appropriately shown in reduced scale, kneels at the entrance of the firechamber (Fig. 74).*

*Busy kitchen scenes like the stone relief from a tomb at Dahuting in Mixian, Henan supply vivid confirmation of the work carried out in an important household of the Eastern Han period. The large stove, with its pots, chimney, and firechamber are clearly shown at an upper corner of the mural, where an attendent loaded with firewood approaches. At another corner, a manservant is apparently ladling out **geng** or stew from a large cauldron. The wealth of the family is revealed by the presence of two meat racks hung with fowl and animals, as well as the ox leg and head on the ground. Meat was a luxury which only the affluent could afford to consume in quantity. Another important item depicted in the Mixian mural is a well with a wooden frame, where a man is shown drawing water. Like the granary and stove, the well constituted an essential installation on the Han estate. Not surprisingly, pottery versions of wells comprised another popular **mingqi** form, buried to supply the deceased with water for all his future needs. Wells employing a pulley system were in common use in the Han period, necessitating a wooden framework over the wellhead to hold the pulleys. Pottery models of wells often look like greatly elongated jars or baskets with tall handles (Fig. 190) or lower curved handles (Fig. 190, 192, 193). This is because the important section of the well which lies below ground level is also depicted.*

Mingqi and the Supernatural

*While even the most mundane aspects of earthly life were reproduced in pottery models, those who made tomb furnishings also had to take cognizance of the unknown world into which the soul of the deceased was entering. The nature of this existence was open to conjecture, unlike the well-ordered Confucian world above ground, where clear precepts and prescribed rituals guided the individual at every step in life. To exercise control over the world of the spirits, and render it more rational and predictable, an elaborate cosmology was evolved by Han scholars. The ancient yinyang theory of complementary opposites was extended to include a system of correspondences which attempted to place natural and supernatural phenomena in a defined context. Thus, the Four Directions or Quadrants of Heaven were linked with the **si shen** – (四神) Dragon, Phoenix, Tiger and Tortoise, embodying the four classes of scaled, feathered, furred and shell-covered creatures. These supernatural beings, two conferred with **yang** (阳) and two with **yin** (阴) attributes, were further linked with the Four Seasons, Four Elements (Wood, Fire, Metal Water) and Four Colours (Green, Red, White, Black). The imaginative recreation of these abstract forces is frequently seen in examples of Han art found in tombs. Visualisations of **si shen** are a recurring theme on lacquered boxes, bronze mirrors, jade plaques as well as pottery sculptures. Undoubtedly, images of the arbiters of the four cosmic directions, like those of other tomb guardians, were considered to be talismanic in nature, employed as deterrents to ward off unwanted visitors.*

Spirits from the next world were generally regarded as powerful but capricious beings with the ability to create mischief. However, even ancestor spirits were considered capable of malevolent actions when displeased. All supernatural beings had to be carefully propitiated with rites and offerings, and precautions of various kinds were taken to keep the tomb free of malignant intervention. "Tomb security jars" employed for assuring the tranquillity of the tomb and family were frequently found in Eastern Han tombs. One such jar unearthed in Xian City, Shaanxi Province carries a humble plea on behalf of the deceased "for a peaceful reception and stay."[23] The practice of using these cinnabar inscribed jars was probably influenced by Daoist concepts relating to the  afterlife,[24] which gained a substantial following among the nobility as well as the masses.

The world was viewed with an incongruous blend of rationality and mysticism by people of all classes. Confucianism, the official ideology, concentrated its attention on the problems of human interaction in this world. It did not attempt to deal with the many insecurities regarding the next world that plagued the individual man. Daoist cults sprang up to fill the spiritual vacuum, offering semi-magical solutions to cope with the question of mortality. People of the Han were willing to place their faith in alchemists who promised immortality through the partaking of gold or cinnabar which had been transmuted into mercury.

The hope of attaining eternal life was also held out by the widespread belief in the existence of the "Isles of the Immortals" (三仙山). Purportedly located in the Eastern Seas, the mountains of these fabled islands were regarded as the abode of fortunate Immortals, happily released from the pains of man's life. For those who had not been able to achieve immortality in their earthly life-span by magical means, various methods of preserving the body and soul could still be resorted to in the tomb. Jade, traditionally associated with purity and indestructibility, was frequently used to stave off decay. It was a common practice to place nephrite cicadas, metaphors for rejuvenation, on the tongue. Princes had whole suits made of jade plaques in an attempt to keep the body intact. This was to help ensure that the **hun** or divine component of the soul would continue to have a home to return to when it wished.

The Han belief in the Isles of the Immortals found visual expression in the decoration of two distinctive tomb ware forms. The motif of mountain peaks rising over waves which symbolises the abode of the Immortals appears in both the cylindrical **lian** (奩) container with a conical-top called the "hill-jar" (Fig. 89, 90, 91, 122, 123) and the **boshanlu** (博山炉) an incense burner referred to as a "vast mountain brazier" (Fig. 117). The Daoist utopia is not presented in these objects as a gentle idyllic landscape, but one with formidably undulating slopes where an incongruous assortment of tigers, hydras, mountain goats, deer, birds and monkeys are engaged in a never-ending chase. It has been suggested that this relentless zoomorphic pursuit was intended to be a visual metaphor for the perpetual force which motivates the cosmos.[25] Interspersed in the moulded friezes on the hill-jar and the **boshanlu** are archers on horses, and clumsy demon-like creatures (Fig. 90). Mountain-climbing men who may be Immortals or virile elders appear occasionally. On a hill-jar described by Laufer[26] two elders make their way through mountains with the help of unusual bird-shaped staffs, which he suggests are depictions of the "pigeon-staves" (鳩杖首) ceremonially presented to Han elders above the age of eighty. Traditionally made of nephrite or bronze, these staffs symbolized a wish for their continuing strength in old age.

Though the function of the hill-jar is not clear, the boshanlu is generally believed to be a receptacle designed for burning incense. The perforations typically seen at the lid or the upper level of the censer permitted the release of aromatic smoke which swirled around the mountains in a clever simulation of clouds and mist at rarified altitudes. Some **boshanlu** have no perforations, however, and may have been used to hold fragrant herbs placed in the tray below. An interesting variant is seen in a lamp-cum-censer (Fig.145) which places the characteristic cone-shaped burner in the midst of four shallow dishes for holding oil.

The multifarious furnishings of the Han tomb were intended to chronicle earthly achievements and display the wealth and possessions of the tomb-owner. Laying in large stocks of grave goods to supply the deceased with food, clothing and other physical needs was also viewed as a paramount filial duty in the furnishing of the tomb. However, the fact that even the most lavishly equipped grave could only serve as the threshold to the unknown was inescapable. It was commonly acknowledged that occult influences surrounded the burial site, necessitating the provision of special articles for propiation and offerings to the supernatural beings which hovered about. Of the varied forms of "spirit articles" placed in the tombs of the period, perhaps it is the ingeniously contrived **boshanlu** that best epitomises both Han hopes for the next life and accompanying fears of the unknown. With its evocative image of the mountainous paradise awaiting the fortunate, this example of **mingqi** serves as a tangible expression of the Han desire to come to terms with the final and inevitable transition of man from one state of existence to another.

(Figures in The Catalogue are referred to in this article)

Notes

[1] Wang Zhongshu, Han Civilisation, K.C.Chang et al.(Trans.), New Haven: Yale University Press, 1982, pp.211–212.
[2] Ibid. p.213.
[3] Rawson, Jessica, Ancient China: Art and Archaeology, London: British Museum, 1980, p.204.
[4] Li Yinde, "The Underground Palace of a Chu Prince at Beidongshan", in Orientations,1990, October, p.58.
[5] Wang Zs., p.181.
[6] Pictured in Treasures from the Han, Singapore: Historical and Cultural Exhibitions Pte. Ltd., 1990, p.67.
[7] Ibid., p.64.
[8] Line from the Odes, quoted by Wheatley, Paul, Pivot of the Four Quarters, Edinburgh : Edinburgh University Press,1971, p.463.
[9] Bodde, Derek, Festivals in Classical China , Princeton: Princeton University Press,1975, p.37, and ch. xviii.
[10] deBary, Wm Theodore (Ed.), Sources of Chinese Tradition, New York and London: Columbia University Press, 1960, p.110.
[11] Watson, Burton, (Trans.), Records of the Historian: Chapters from the Shih Chi of Ssu-ma Ch"ien , New York: Columbia University Press, 1969, p.350.
[12] An unusual specimen with a pronounced iridescent exterior, but retaining the original dark green glaze within its mouth, is seen in Fig. 167 in the exhibition.
[13] Wang Zs,p.179.
[14] Wang Z.s., p.60.
[15] Yu Yingshih, in Chang Kwang-chih (Ed.), Food in Chinese Culture: Anthropological and Historical Perspectives, New Haven: Yale University Press, 1977, pp.68–69.
[16] Ho Judy .Chunghwa.,"Art and Context: Chinese Ceramic Sculpture", in Orientations, 1989, November, p. 63.
[17] Vollmer, Keall and Nagai-Berthrong, Silk Roads, China Ships, Toronto: Royal Ontario Museum, 1983 , p.23.
[18] Quoted by Bodde, p.154.
[19] Ibid. p.159.
[20] Yu Ys. in K.C.Chang (Ed)(1977),p. 57.
[21] Wang Zs,p.146.
[22] Laufer, Berthold, Chinese Pottery of the Han Dynasty, Rutland, Vermont: Charles. E. Tuttle Co., 1962, p.79.
[23] Treasures from the Han,p.67.
[24] Wang Zs., p.210.
[25] Li Yinde, "A Han Bronze Mirror" in Orientations, 1990, October, p.75.
[26] Laufer,B.(1962), pp.205–206.

Selected Bibliography

Bodde, Derk, Festivals in Classical China, Princeton University Press, 1975.
Chang Kwang-chih (Ed.), Food in Chinese Culture: Anthropological and Historical Perspectives, New Haven; Yale University Press, 1977.
Clarke, Basil (Ed.), Chinese Science and the West, London: Nile and Mackenzie and FEP International, 1980
de Bary, Wm. Theodore (Ed.) Sources of Chinese Tradition, Vol 1 N.Y, and London: Columbia University Press, 1960

Dien, Albert E., "Chinese Beliefs in the Afterworld", *The Quest for Eternity: Chinese Ceramic Sculptures from the People's Republic of China*, San Francisco: Los Angeles County Museum of Art and Chronicle Books, 1987.
Eberhard, Wolfram, *A History of China*, Berkeley and Los Angeles: University of California Press, 1969.
Fitzgerald, C.P., *Barbarian Beds: Origin of the Chair in China*, London: The Cresset Press, 1965.
_____, *China. A Short Cultural History*, London: Cresset Press, 1958.
Fu Qifeng, *Chinese Acrobatics Through the Ages*, translated by Ouyang Caiwei and Rhoda Stockwell, Beijing: Foreign Languages Press, 1985.
Ho, Judy Chunghwa, "Art and Context: Chinese Ceramic Sculpture", *Orientations*, 1989, November, pp. 62–69.
Hunan sheng bowuguan, Zhongguo kexueyuan kaogu yanjiusuo, *Changsha Mawangdui yihao Han mu*, 2 vol. Peking: Wenwu chubanshe, 1973.
Kwok Man Ho, Martin Palmer and Joanne O'Brien, *The Fortune Teller's I Ching*, New York: Ballantine Books, 1986.
Laufer, Berthold, *Chinese Pottery of the Han Dynasty*. Rutland, Vermont: Charles E. Tuttle Company, 1962.
Le Blanc, Charles, *Huai Nan Tzu, Philosophical Synthesis in Early Han Thought*, Hongkong: Hongkong University Press, 1985.
Li Hui-lin, *Nan-fang Ts'ao Mu Chuang: A Fourth Century Flora of S.E. Asia*, Hongkong: The Chinese University Press, 1979.
Li Yinde, "The Underground Palace of a Chu Prince at Beidongshan," *Orientations*, 1990, October, pp.57–61.
_____, "A Han Bronze Mirror", *Orientations*, 1990, October, pp. 74–75.
Rawson, Jessica, *Ancient China: Art and Archaelogy*, London: British Museum, 1980.
Records of the Historian, Chapters from the Shih Chi of Ssu-ma Chien translated by Burton Watson, New York: Columbia University Press, 1969.
Steinhardt, Nancy S. et al., *Chinese Traditional Architecture*, New York: Chinese Institute in America, 1984.
Tang Shixin, "Han Pictorial Stone Carvings", *Orientations*, 1990, October, pp. 67–73.
Thorpe, R.L. and Bower, V., *Spirit and Ritual, The Morse Collection of Ancient Chinese Art*, Metropolitan Museum of Art, 1982.
Thorpe, Robert L., "The Qin and Han Imperial Tombs and the Development of Mortuary Architecture', *The Quest for Eternity: Chinese Ceramic Sculptures from the People's Republic of China*, San Francisco: Los Angeles Country Museum of Art and Chronicle Books, 1987.
Treasures from the Han, Singapore: Historical and Cultural Exhibitions Pte Ltd., 1990.
Vollmer, Keall and Nagai-Berthrong, *Silk Roads, China Ships*, Toronto: Royal Ontarion Museum, 1983.
Wang Renbo, "General Comments on Chinese Funerary Sculpture", *The Quest for Eternity: Chinese Ceramic Sculptures from the People's Republic of China*, San Francisco: Los Angeles Country Museum of Art and Chronicle Books, 1987.
Wang Zhongshu, *Han Civilisation*. Translated by K.C. Chang et al. New Haven: Yale University Press, 1982.
Watt, J.C.Y., *A Han Tomb in Lei Cheng Uk*, Hongkong: Urban Council, 1983.
Wheatley, Paul, *Pivot of the Four Quarters*, Edinburgh: Edinburgh University Press, 1971.
Willetts, William, *Chinese Art*, vol 1, Penguin Books, 1958.

ENG–LEE SEOK CHEE

Received her higher education in the U.S.A with a B.A. degree in Art History from Smith College, Northampton, Mass. and M.A. degree in teaching of Art from Columbia University.

She joined the National Museum Singapore in 1977 as an Assistant Curator. From August 1980 to March 1991 she assumed responsibilities as Curator for the Chinese Collections. She designed a number of exhibitions for the museum, which revolved around the theme of ceramics, including "Chinese Teaware and Utensils", "Kendi and Kraak: Saga of the Ceramic Trade" and "The Enterprising Potter."

Recently retired from her position as Senior Curator she continues to be affiliated with the National Museum in an advisory capacity.

The Interchange of Motifs and the Development of Realism in the Decorative Arts of the Han

by Rosemary E. Scott

In any study of the decorative arts of the Han period, two often interlinked aspects of their design become immediately apparent. Firstly, it can be seen that there was considerable interchange of decorative motifs and themes between the objects made in different materials, and secondly, realism was increasingly employed in the depiction of those motifs and themes. Regional variations and the influence of minority peoples on the decorative arts are, of course, also important, but are beyond the scope of this paper.

The interchange of major decorative themes between the different materials will be illustrated during the later discussions in this paper, but it is perhaps of almost equal importance that a number of the minor motifs seen on the decorative arts of the Han period are also transferred from one medium to another. This first came to my attention in the late 1970s while examining the origins of designs on Han lacquer wares.[1] The minor band made up of extended lozenges seen on **lian** *boxes such as that in the British Museum, London (Fig. i) and other vessels did not seem an obvious one to be developed by the lacquer painter. With the publication of the silk textiles (in excellent condition) from tomb number one at Mawangdui, however, the source of this design became clear.[2] Amongst the figured silks from this tomb were several into which this same*

i

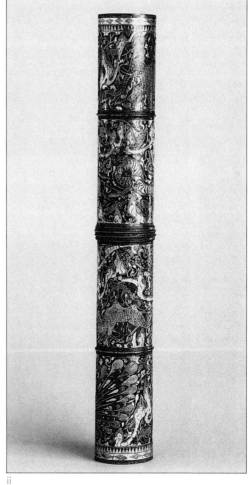

ii

extended lozenge design had been woven, and such a design is of course one much more readily devised by the weaver than the lacquer painter. A somewhat simpler version of this lozenge design has also been found on inlaid bronzes such as the chariot fitting excavated from the tomb of Prince Kang at Dingxian in Hebei province in 1965[3], and a similar fitting recently exhibited in London (Fig. ii)[4]. It is most probable that while the lacquer painter was influenced by the weaver's design, the bronze worker fashioned his inlaid gold and silver design from the lacquer prototype.

Another aspect of the decoration on the British Museum **lian** also found its way onto vessels in other materials. The silver quatrefoil inlaid into the lacquer on the cover of the **lian** is similar to that seen on a number of lacquer boxes. It can, however also be seen on a several gilt bronze vessels[5] and in addition appears on ceramic copies of such vessels as in the case of the green-glazed example in the current exhibition (Fig. 98). The source of this design is almost certainly floral, and while the flattened, formal design on the lacquer, gilt bronze and ceramic vessels usually has four 'petals' (three in the case of horse-shoe shaped boxes), a very similar but more naturalistic floral form can be seen on bronze finials decorated with six petals of gold and silver inlay or gilding, such as that excavated from tomb number one at Mancheng in Hebei province in 1968[6].

As far as the major decorative themes are concerned, the most important development was the increasingly realistic depiction of some of the chosen motifs. The pertinent dictionary definition of **realism** is given as "... fidelity of representation, rendering the precise details of the real thing or scene ...". There are those, therefore, who will argue that it is not possible to describe mythological creatures such as dragons, and intangible figures like Daoist immortals as being realistically depicted. The same problem of linguistics occurs with any attempt to apply terms such as naturalistic or life-like. How then are we to describe the change that took place in the decorative arts during the latter part of the Bronze Age in China? For change, there was, from the decorative style of the Shang and Western Zhou periods which sacrificed life-like portrayal to formalized design, to the fully developed, 'realistic' style of the Eastern Han period.

In this change to realistic representation in the later Bronze Age, one of the most significant features is the development of landscape, which once again can be seen on objects made in many different materials and forms. The two most common forms are the three-dimensional **boshan** [magic mountain] jars and censers produced in lead-glazed earthenware (Fig. 89, 90, 91, 117, 122, 123) and inlaid bronze such as that from the tomb of Liu Sheng, Prince of Zhongshan, at Mancheng, Hobei province[7] (Fig. iv), and the two-dimensional linear landscapes like those painted on lacquer vessels such as the **lian** [toilet box],

iii

excavated at Jiangling and dated to the Warring States period[8] as well as that in the British Museum (Fig. i) discussed above. Most of the **boshan** jars indeed combine both types of landscape depiction, having lids in high three-dimensional moulded relief, and more linear depictions in low relief around the bases. The three dimensional lids are clearly mountains, but the linear depictions are less easy to identify.

The forms of these two-dimensional landscapes are somewhat amorphous, sometimes appearing cloud-like, or resembling waves and at other times having a more solid, rocky appearance. Perhaps the finest of the cloud-like depictions can be seen on one of the coffins from tomb number one at Mawangdui (Fig. iii). These multicoloured forms have their outlines and scrolling details drawn in slight relief giving a very rich appearance to the surface of the coffin. They provide a 'landscape' for various creatures and immortals which are painted in a very lively and occasionally amusing fashion. These creatures, some of whom can be identified from the text of the **Shan hai jing**, are by no means randomly placed among these 'landscape' forms, but, instead, gallop across or, peer around the 'landscape', and casually sit upon them. However vapourously the forms are painted, the creatures that inhabit them interact with them as if they were solid.

iv

Another cloud or wave-like form of landscape is seen on painted lacquer and also on inlaid bronze and on textiles of the Han period. This form seems ultimately to derive from the scrolling, but articulated dragon forms of the Warring States period, such as those seen on the lacquered leather shields of the Chu state. It can be seen at its most accomplished on an inlaid bronze **boshan** censer excavated in 1968 from the tomb of Prince Liu Sheng at Mancheng in Hebei province (Fig. iv) Here the cloud and wave forms are used to enhance the already three-dimensional landscape. They are however similarly used on flat surfaces in lacquer and textiles, where they alone provide an indication of the landscape setting.

An undulating linear landscape which hovers somewhere between the wave and mountain form can be seen on painted lacquers, bronzes and textiles. Its painted lacquer form can be seen on the lid of the British Museum **lian** (Fig. i), while an example in woven textile is among the Eastern Han materials in the Xinjiang Archaeological Research Institute (Fig. v). The textile example is interesting in that the design not only includes animals and equestrian figures (as is usually the case and will be discussed later) but also includes auspicious characters **zhang le ming guang** as part of the decoration. The use of characters is usually confined to the textile version of this motif in the Han period.

This undulating wave-like form of landscape is, of course, also seen on the ceramic wares. It appears on a number of the **boshan** jars in the exhibition and also in the hunting scenes moulded on the shoulders of **hu** vessels glazed in either green or amber (Fig. 83, 84, 95), Fig. 83 being a particularly clear example.

The most convincing depictions of mountains on vessels, apart from the three dimensional **boshan** vessels are those seen on the inlaid bronze objects such as the chariot fitting (Fig. ii). All the landscapes discussed above are full of movement, both in terms of the creatures that inhabit them and in terms of their own forms. There is, however, a group of objects on which much more static, but arguably more realistic landscapes appear. These are moulded tomb bricks from Sichuan province (Fig. vi). The landscape examples usually depict some feature of everyday life - hunting, salt production etc. The mountains are shown as rough cone shapes, but there is an attempt at the suggestion of recession by placing the mountains one behind another.

The landscapes of the Han decorative arts usually provide a setting for animals, humans or immortals, who are depicted with increasing realism during this period. Many of the decorations show hunting scenes with leaping animals and chasing horsemen. The horsemen are often drawing their bows while turning around in the saddle in a stance called the Parthian shot. The precise identity of these scenes has been the subject of considerable debate amongst scholars, as has been the choice of animals[9]. These animals are often a mixture of the real and mythical, but are always shown in very life-like manner. It has been suggested that some of these animals are representative of auspicious omens **xiangrui** acting as intermediaries between

v

heaven and earth. Some of the animals were never or were no longer indigenous to China by the time the items were produced, and may represent gifts received by the powerful Han empire from other countries, the elephant and the camel shown on the chariot fitting (Fig. ii) are two examples. The hunting scenes may well depict the imperial hunts carefully stage-managed in the royal parks. Also popular decorative motifs during the later Bronze Age are the animals that represent the four quarters - the Green Dragon of the East, the White Tiger of the West, the Vermillion Bird of the South and the Dark Warrior (tortoise/snake) of the North. Certain animals and birds were, in addition, associated with particular rituals and beliefs. The owl (Fig. 88, 30) for instance is often seen among funerary pottery vessels and is associated with calling the soul of the dead. An owl is also depicted on the painted banner which was placed over the coffin in tomb number one at Mawangdui[10]

Some animals might almost have been designed with the decorator in mind, and in Warring States and Han periods full advantage was taken of this. The most obvious example is the tiger, which, as we have already seen on the chariot fitting (Fig. ii) could be depicted with great realism while still taking full advantage of the decorative quality of the striped skin. Another example on which the tiger form was used is a bronze tally inlaid with gold found in the tomb of the King of Nan Yue (contemporaneous with the early Western Han period)[11]. Here the tiger is shown snarling and ready to spring. It is however more usually depicted in motion with head and tail up, and all four legs powering it forward. In this case the head back and tail form a 'C' or 'U' shape, which provides further possibilities for the decorator. One of these animated tigers was inlaid in silver into the lid of the lacquer **lian** in the British Museum (Fig. i), but it is now no longer possible to see if the markings were shown in detail. They are clearly to be seen, however, on the circular moulded ceramic eaves-end tiles from the site of the Weiyang Palace of the first Han emperor, now in the Shaanxi Provincial Museum (Fig vii). At first glance it might be thought that the stance of the tiger had been distorted in order to make it fit

vii

vi

into the circular shape of the tile although it does not appear unnatural. In fact we can see a tiger in the same pose on a Warring States embroidery (Fig. viii). In the latter case there is no reason of space for the adoption of this particular form, which appears at once both decorative and surprisingly natural. The embroidery which is worked entirely in chain-stitch also uses appropriate black and amber thread to depict the stripes of the animal.

Felines of course had been seen in a number of forms, but seem to have reached their peak of popularity in the Han period, as well as their most naturalistic depiction. In addition to tigers, leopards also provided the craftsman with an ideal subject in terms of form and pattern of skin. Perhaps the most famous examples are the leopard weights excavated from the tomb of Princess Dou Wan at Mancheng, Hebei province (Fig. ix). These four leopards with their garnet eyes and gilded coats are in naturalistic poses, although certain artistic license has been taken with the markings of the skin to make them even more decorative.

Unlike the other depictions of animals discussed above these leopards are small in-the-round sculptures, and as such are typical of the realism developed in Han sculpture. Looking back to the early Bronze Age, even the famous elephant **zun** of the Shang period[12] which have a realistic basic shape are covered in relief elements - flanges, **leiwen** [thunder pattern] and other designs that bear no relation to their natural appearance. We may contrast with these elephant **zun** vessels not only small sculptures like the leopards, but vessels such as the bovine **zun** excavated from a Western Han tomb at Sanlidun, Lianshui country in Jiangsu province, and normally dated to the late Warring States period (Fig. x). The shape of this latter creature is wholly naturalistic, even to its slightly cocked head and enquiring expression. Although it is elaborately decorated with gold and silver inlay designs, these have not been allowed to disturb the outlines and detract from the realism of the piece. The Han dynasty ceramic animals in the current exhibition are a further manifestation of this trend, and it is significant that many of the funerary animals made in the Han period are simple, naturalistically modelled domestic animals - dogs, ducks, chickens, pigs, sheep etc. They are even shown in some cases in a domestic setting, pigs in their sty, sheep in their enclosure, and dogs wearing their collars. These figures provide a complete contrast with the rather grand animals found in Tang dynasty tombs some centuries later.

One animal found in both Han and Tang tombs, however, is the horse, and in both periods it is depicted with care and realism. Its inclusion among the Han animals is scarcely surprising, for it is at this time that the famous Ferghana horses were first introduced into China. The best known in-the-round Han horse is the so-called flying horse of Gansu (Fig.

viii

xi) excavated at Wuwei in Gansu province. Not only is this horse wonderfully realistically depicted, but it is a triumph of the bronze caster's artistry as it does, on a single hoof, balance on the back of a swallow. There are, however, many two-dimensional depictions of horses dating to the Han period which display equal life and movement. Some of these are to be seen on painted tomb bricks from sites such as Jiayuguan in Gansu, where they are shown being ridden and also harnessed to chariots[13]. In both cases they are shown as powerful, spirited animals. The same can be said of those depicted on moulded bricks like those in the current

ix

exhibition (Fig. 11, 12), and in stone relief carvings such as those from Sunjiacun, Teng county, Shandong province.

Similar developments towards a new realism can be seen in the depiction of human figures. The human figure occurred relatively infrequently in the early Bronze Age: the human faces on the four-legged **ding** excavated at Ningxiang, Hunan province in 1965[14], those human figures entering the jaws of a mythical beast, and the kneeling jade figure from Fu Hao's tomb being exceptions rather than the rule. Perhaps the most famous of the realistic human figures to be unearthed in recent years are those that made up the buried army of the First Qin Emperor[15]. The wide range of in-the-round ceramic human figures in this exhibition are evidence of the extent to which this theme of realistic human figure depiction developed in the Han period. Equally realistic figures have also been found in gilt bronze such as the lamp excavated from the tomb of

x

Princess Dou Wan at Mancheng, Hebei province, while the wooden figures with real silk or painted clothing from tombs like those at Mawangdui are less sophisticated but nevertheless attempt a kind of realism.

Two dimensional depictions of human figures (on horseback or otherwise) dating to the Han period abound on painted tomb bricks, moulded bricks, stone relief carvings, inlaid into lacquer, inlaid into bronze, and even on the Mawangdui banner mentioned above, as well as the famous tomb murals. One of the most interesting examples of figure painting on a decorative art object, however, is on a lidded basket, painted in lacquer which was excavated from the so-called 'tomb of the painted basket'

xi

at the Han Commandary of Lolang in Korea (Fig. xii). More than ninety figures are shown around the edges of this basket. Each one is identified and is shown with individual characteristics, and despite the limitations of space the lacquer artist has managed to group and incline the figures as if in conversation.

In both two and three-dimensional items in many different materials the decorative arts of the later Bronze Age and

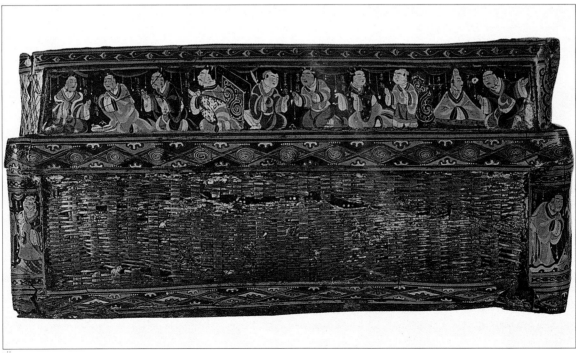
xii

particularly those of the Han period are characterized by an increasing degree of realism in the depiction of animals, birds, humans and immortals. This was however achieved without losing any of the decorative effect of these remarkable objects.

(Figures in The Catalogue are referred to in this article)

Notes

1. Rosemary Scott, 'The earliest Chinese Lacquer', Lacquerwork in Asia and Beyond, Colloquies on Art & Archaeology in Asia No. 11, (ed. W. Watson), 1982, pp. 1-17.
2. Mawangdui yihao Han mu, Wenwu chubanshe, Beijing 1973, vol. 2, plates 121, 122, 137, 139 etc.
3. The Genius of China, (ed.) William Watson, The Royal Academy, London, 1973, no. 173.
4. Eskenazi, Inlaid bronze and related material from pre-Tang China, London, 1991, no. 16.
5. Qian Hao et al., Out of China's Earth, London, 1981, pl. 212.
6. Mancheng Han mu fajue bao gao, Beijing, 1980, vol. 1, pl. 50, fig. 2.
7. Xin Zhongguo chutu wenwu [Historical Relics Unearthed in New China], Foreign Languages Press, Beijing, 1972, plate 98.
8. Hubei Jiangling san zuo Chu mou chutu pi zhong yao wenwu, no. 4, 1974, pp. 33.
9. Wu Hung, 'A Sanpan Shan Chariot Ornament and the Xiangrui Design in Western Han Art', Archives of Asian Art, vol. 37, New York, 1984, pp. 38-59.
   Jacobson, E., 'Mountains and Nomads: A Reconstruction of the Origins of Chinese Landscape Representation'. Bulletin of the Museum of Far Eastern Antiquities, vol. 57, Stockholm, pp. 133-180.
10. Mawangdui yihao mu, op. cit., plate 76.
11. Swart, P.,'The Tomb of the King of Nan Yue', Orientations, June 1990, fig. 19.
12. Pope, Gettens, Cahill & Barnard, The Freer Gallery Bronzes, vol. 1, plate 40.
13. Chuka Jimmin Kyowakoku shutsudo bumbutsu ten (exhibition), Tokyo & Kyotot, 1973, p. 34.
14. Watson, W. (ed.), The Genius of China, The Royal Academy, London, 1973, no. 79.
15. Wenwu chubanshe, Beijing, 1983.

ROSEMARY E. SCOTT

Took a degree in the Art and Archaeology of China at the School of Oriental and African Studies, University of London, where she went on to do post-graduate research into early Chinese Lacquer. She was Deputy Keeper of the Burrell Collection, Glasgow, with curatorial responsibility for the Oriental material before taking up her present post as Curator of the Percival David Foundation of Chinese Art. She also teaches Chinese art at the University of London and has published books and articles on a number of aspects of the Chinese decorative arts. Her main areas of research are ceramics, lacquer and textiles. She has travelled widely in China.

Tall Pottery Towers and their Archaeological Contexts

by Candace J. Lewis

"Northwest the tall tower stands, its top level with floating clouds, patterned windows webbed in lattice, roofs piled three storeys high. From above, the sound of strings and song; what sadness in that melody? Who could play a tune like this, who but the wife of Qi Liang?..."
(From one of the Nineteen Old Poems of the Eastern Han dynasty, translated by Burton Watson[1])

In the high tower with forecourt (Fig. 185), a single form reaches upwards, roofs piled high. The windows are latticed, the roofs decorated with ornamental flower-shaped end tiles. At each of the three upper storeys, a single figure sits in the opening. Chinese archaeologists frequently interpret a single figure "gazing into the distance" as a depiction of the owner of the tomb. Is one of these figures — the one at the centre in the official's cap — the master of the tomb? Is this tower, and the three other tall towers in this exhibition (Fig. 184, 186 and 188), a recreation of the vision presented in the contemporary poem? Perhaps. The answers to these questions are not yet clear. A more complete archaeological picture of pottery tall towers, however, is beginning to emerge. It is the subject of discussion in this essay[2].

Tall pottery towers were created during the Eastern Han dynasty (AD 25–220). Along with other **mingqi** (burial objects), they were intended to be placed inside the tomb to accompany the deceased into the after-life. The four towers in this exhibition (Fig. 184, 185, 186, and 188) represent variations of a type which has been excavated in China. All four towers are made of red clay which was covered with a copper-lead glaze and fired to earthenware temperatures. All were created during Eastern Han, probably during the second century. They can be associated with examples excavated in China in a region centering on western Henan Province. This essay attempts to place the towers in the larger context of excavations throughout China and in the smaller context of their placement within the tomb.

Farmhouse
Eastern Han.........Red earthenware with traces of pigment
ht: 22.9 cm

From the Schloss Collection, New York. Photograph by Sarah Wells, courtesy of the Vassar College Art Gallery

Excavations of architectural models throughout China

Tombs containing architectural models, some very large and elaborate, have been excavated all over China. Examples have been found in the north: in Hebei, Henan, and Shaanxi Provinces; in the south: in Hubei, Hunan, Jiangsu, Anhui, Guangxi and Guangdong Provinces, and even as far west as the relatively isolated region of Sichuan.[3] There is a marked difference between the architectural models from northern and southern China. In general, the models from southern China are only one or two storeys high and comprised a simple house with an attached courtyard or a courtyard complex. They are frequently made of unglazed red earthenware, sometimes with added pigments. The examples from northern China, in contrast, seem deliberately to avoid representing the courtyard arrangement (thought to have comprised all architectural compounds in ancient China). The tomb models from northern China represent single tall towers.

There are a few exceptions, of course. A detailed courtyard model was discovered in a tomb from Laodaosi in Shaanxi Province, in northern China, for example.[4] There is an interesting tall tower with green glaze which was found in Xiangyang, Hubei, in southern China.[5] Nevertheless, it can be stated that, generally, models in the form of courtyard complexes come from southern China, while models of single tall towers come from the north.

In the South

The small farmhouse from the Schloss collection in New York (Fig. A) is typical of models discovered in southern China. Only 22.9 cm. tall, it is a depiction of an L-shaped house with a courtyard in the rear (not shown in the photograph). Inside the courtyard is a model of a sleeping dog. The architecture is relatively simple: a wooden framed structure, two storeys high, with open lattice work, possibly for ventilation in the warm southern climate. Traces of red and black pigments remain on the tiled roof. In the front, standing with out-stretched arms, near the door, is a figure, perhaps the master of the house. Many such works have been found in graves throughout the Yangtze River region. It is similar to examples found in the region of Changsha, Hunan Province.[6]

A dated model of considerable interest has been discovered further south at tomb no. 2, Ma ying gang, at the Zoological Gardens in Guangzhou, Guangdong Province. The unglazed model of a manor-house has been dated AD 76.[7] This example, more elaborate than the farmhouse (Fig. A), depicts an architectural complex enclosing two small houses within its courtyard. The manor-house has high walls with gates at the front and back and six watch-towers. Eleven figures of people and one of a horse are included. The model is 29.6 cm. high.

Courtyard House with a Tower. excavated at Yunmeng, Hubei in 1979
Eastern Han dynasty..........Red earthenware with green glaze
ht: 72 cm

From Cultural Relics Bureau of the Ministry of Culture and the Palace Museum eds., Quanguo Chutu Wenwu Zhenpin Chuan 1976-1984 (A Selection of the Treasure of Archaeological Finds of China 1976-1984), 1985, pl. 29

C

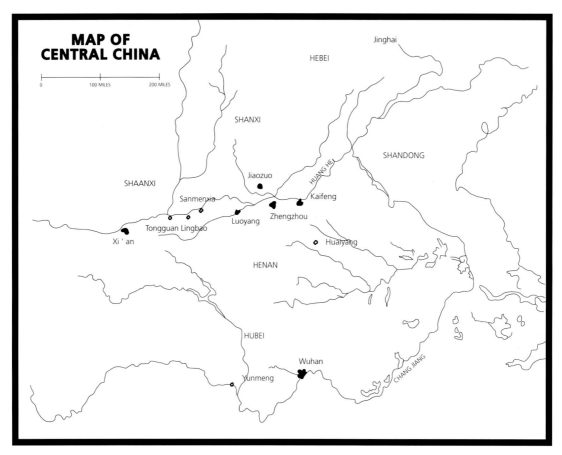

B. *Map of central China, showing sections of Shaanxi, Shanxi, Henan, Hubei, and Shandong Provinces*

A third example of the southern style was excavated further to the north, from an Eastern Han tomb at Yunmeng, near Jiangling, Hubei on the bank of the Yangtze River (see map in Fig. B).[8] The pottery castle (Fig. C), like the farmhouse and the manor-house discussed, demonstrates an emphasis on a total complex – here including a courtyard, an entrance building, a detached watch booth, and a tower. The inclusion of a tower, as well as the use of a thin wash of green lead glaze over the red clay, suggests some influence from the neighboring regions of Henan to the north. This representation of a manor-house is taller than the examples discussed above; it is 72 cm. tall. Its height also suggests influence from the north. Nevertheless, the model is a representation of a whole complex and can be considered exemplary of the southern style.

In the North

The architectural models of buildings found in northern China stand in striking contrast to those of the south. A very large proportion of the tombs of the Eastern Han period are equipped with tall pottery towers. The towers appear in a variety of models, all of which share the one characteristic of great height. In addition, the prominence of the tower as the main architectural element is evident. All other structures-courtyards, gates, walls, watch-towers, and subsidiary buildings – are reduced in size or eliminated.

One of the most spectacular pottery towers is a multi-storeyed structure from Jinghai in Hebei Province (Fig. D). Refer to the map in Fig. B[9]. The tower is four storeys high, square in cross-section with four symmetrically placed ramps at the bottom. It is very tall – 136 cm., with highly detailed roofs and bracketing[10]. Models of small birds rest in the eaves.

Height is stressed also in two towers from Henan Province. The first (Fig. E) is a magnificent edifice which was excavated in 1972 from a tomb in the western suburbs of Jiaozuo in Henan[11]. The tower has been identified as a storehouse. At the front gate, a small figure with a sack of grain on his back raises a foot to enter the courtyard. The presence of a figure "gazing into the distance" on the top level, as well as the courtyard with watchdog, the entrance gate with flanking towers, the many storeys with tiled roofs, windows, and complex bracketing, suggest that this structure represents more than just a granary. The tower is made of grey earthenware and has been painted with pigments to create beautiful surface designs.

The other example was found in 1954 in Huaiyang County, Henan (Fig. D). The tower is made of red clay with a green glaze, now much destroyed after burial. This is a very odd work. It is a thin, tall tower, three storeys high, with roofs covered with birds. At the bottom is a figure identified as a guard accompanied by four figures carrying grain. On each of the upper levels are beds, one of the few depictions of a bed in ancient China. The architectural structure is the most peculiar. Under the eaves are columns in the shape of nude male and female figures. They are accompanied by complicated, even fanciful, bracketing. At the base of each level, built into the architecture are small busts of human figures. The use of the human figure, especially nude, is unprecedented in known examples of architectural models or in two-dimensional representations of architecture in ancient China.

The four towers in this exhibition (Fig. 184, 185, 186 and 188) are close in style to several tall towers found in western Henan Province. The first excavated model, a green-glazed tower in a moat made of red earthenware (Fig. F), was discovered in 1958 at Sanshengwan in Lingbao County of western Henan[12]. The symmetrical pavilion is animated by hand-modelled figures. At the four corners are soldiers holding crossbows; in the center is a single figure standing erect; and on the top level a figure raises a wine cup to his mouth to drink. The size and style of this piece is very similar to two towers in moats in this exhibition (Fig. 184 and 188). The tower from Sanshengwan, Lingbao (Fig. F) is 64 cm. high, while the two towers in this exhibition (Fig. 184 and 188) are 69 cm. and 85 cm. high. All three are towers in round basins; all are made of red earthenware with green glaze; and all have simple roofs with almost no indication of bracketing. The porches at the upper levels have horizontal cut-out designs.

These towers can also be associated with two towers in basins found in tombs in Shanxian County[13], thus a proposed origin in western Henan for the two towers in this exhibition (Fig. 184 and 188) seems reasonable. The excavated works have been dated to the Eastern Han period. A similar date is suggested for the two towers here.

In 1972, four large Eastern Han tombs were excavated

Tower excavated in Hebei Province
Eastern Han.........Red earthenware with glaze
ht: 136 cm

From Cultural Relics Bureau of the Ministry of Culture and the Palace Museum eds., Quanguo Chutu Wenwu Zhenpin Chuan 1976-1984 (A Selection of the Treasure of Archaeological Finds of China 1976-1984), 1985, pl. 28

D

TALL POTTERY TOWERS

Tower excavated at Jiaozuo, Henan
Eastern Han.........Grey earthenware with slip and pigments
ht: 134 cm

From Henan Provincial Museum, Henan Sheng Bowuguan, Zhongguo Bowuguan Cong Shu, vol. 7, Wenwu Press, 1982, no. 73

E

at Zhangwan, in Lingbao County, Henan, the same county where the tower in a moat (Fig. F) discussed above was found. The tombs were rich in their furnishings. Among them was a tall water pavilion resting in a square basin (Fig. G). It was found in a side chamber of tomb no. 3. Made of red earthenware with a green lead glaze, the tower is remarkable for its lively depiction of a three-storey structure complete with **dougong** bracketing, tile roofs with decorative florette end tiles, and latticed windows. The building is covered with mould-made figures – musicians, guards with crossbows, officials, a single figure in the doorway of the second level "gazing into the distance", and water animals such as ducks, fish, and turtles. This tower is dated by archaeologists to the end of the Eastern Han dynasty (AD 25–220), probably late second century. In addition, the archaeologists have found inscriptions in the tombs mentioning "Yang". Therefore, they speculate that this tomb was one of a cluster of tombs belonging to the Yang family. Yang was the dominant clan in Hongnong Prefecture of the Eastern Han (in modern day western Henan and part of neighboring Shaanxi).

The three-storey tower in this exhibition (Fig. 186) is astonishingly similar to the excavated tower from Zhangwan, Lingbao. Like the excavated work, the tower is made of red clay with a green glaze. Rising tall and thin from a square courtyard (rather than a pool), the tower has similar door openings, latticed windows, bracketing, tile roofs with florette end tiles, and lively figures. The figures in this case are hand-modelled, not mould-made. The tower discussed above (Fig. 185) also shares many of the same characteristics. Like the excavated tower from Zhangwan, Lingbao, which is 130 cm. high, these two towers in the exhibition are also tall (Fig. 185: 110 cm., Fig. 186: 104 cm.). The tallest example of this type in a collection outside of China may be the tower in the Schloss collection (Fig. H) at 144.8 cm. (just three inches shy of five feet).

All four towers in this exhibition, therefore, can be matched with excavated works. The two smaller towers in round basins (Fig. 184 and 188), are similar to works excavated from Shanxian and Lingbao

F

TOWER IN A BASIN (water pavilion). Excavated from Sanshengwan, Lingbao county, Henan in 1958
Eastern Han..........Red earthenware with green glaze
ht: 64 cm

From Henan Provincial Museum, Henan Sheng Bowuguan, Zhongguo Bowuguan Cong Shu, vol. 7, Wenwu Press, 1982, no. 76

Counties in western Henan (Fig. F). The other two taller towers (Fig. 185 and 186) can be associated with examples excavated at Zhangwan, Lingbao County, Henan. The relationship between these two groups of works is not known. Were they made at different times during the Eastern Han? Were they made in different workshops? Were they made for different clientele? It is evident, however, that all of these towers were made during the latter part of the Eastern Han period, probably during the second century AD, and all were made in an area centering on western Henan.

Towers in the context of the tomb

At the end of the Western Han dynasty (206 BC-AD 9), during the Wang Mang interregnum (AD 8–25), and during the Eastern Han dynasty (AD 25–220), the power of great families became increasingly important in Chinese society. The common farmers had a very difficult task in producing enough food on their lands to supply their own needs and for taxes. In addition, each farmer was required to provide corvee labor to the state. As a result, many simple farming families were forced into bankruptcy, sometimes continuing to live on the land as tenant farmers or hired laborers serving the great family of the neighborhood[14]. In this fashion, the large families in manorial estates expanded their holdings and their wealth.

This phenomenon is expressed in the archaeological record in the appearance of many more tombs belonging to the wealthy families dating to the Eastern Han period. These tombs, unlike the royal tombs of the Western Han or even of the Eastern Han period, were of intermediate size. They were built of small fired bricks, constructed into multi-chambered tombs with vaulted ceilings. In addition, they were usually made for more than one person, and were stocked with a generous supply of grave goods.

Unlike the tombs of the aristocracy and royalty of the Western Han, which included an enormous number of luxury items from everyday life, these more modest tombs of the the Eastern Han gentry were stocked with a supply of replicas of the essentials of everyday life to be taken into the after-life. These objects were made predominantly of clay. Among them, the largest and most detailed were the tall pottery towers.

Although the four towers in this exhibition are without provenance, they can be matched with excavated examples. One tomb provides a very good example of the type of tomb in which these four towers would originally have been placed. The tower in Fig. G was found in tomb no. 3 at Zhangwan, Lingbao County, Henan (Fig. I). The tomb is a vaulted underground structure made of fired rectangular bricks. It is composed of three rooms with an entrance ramp descending from the east. At the entrance to the front chamber were found, first, a small pottery jar and, behind it, two tall lamps. Among the other items found in the front chamber were a guardian dog, several granaries, machines for processing grain, stoves, a censer, and a very lively depiction of two men playing

Tall Tower excavated from Tomb 3 at Zhangwan, Lingbao county, Henan in 1973.
Eastern Han dynasty, second century.........Red earthenware with green glaze
ht: 130 cm

From Henan Provincial Museum, Henan Sheng Bowuguan, Zhongguo Bowuguan Cong Shu, vol. 7, Wenwu Press, 1982, no. 77

G

the game of **liu bo**. All were made of red pottery.

In the side chamber, to the south, were found the tall water pavilion (Fig. G). Also in this chamber were a model of a farmer holding a spade, a well, a pig-sty, a goats' pen, a pair of candlesticks, and two broken pottery vessels.

In the rear chamber, there were fewer tomb furnishings. One of the most remarkable in the tomb was found there, however. It is a pottery table with a green glaze. The pottery container on top of it was connected to the table by the fusion of the glaze in the kiln. A pottery **lian** container was also found in this chamber. At the rear of the chamber were two coffins (Fig. I).

While it is not possible to ascertain all the beliefs of the people who built tombs such as the one at Zhangwan, Lingbao, it is possible to conclude that some of the aspects of everyday life on a manorial estate were considered essential to accompany the soul of the deceased into the after-life. Light was always present in the form of pottery lamps. The critical symbols of sustenance, such as the stove, the granary, and the well, were always included as pottery replicas. The pottery tower was placed in the front or side tomb chamber with replicas of the other structures of the estate. The function and meaning of the pottery tower is still open to debate, but it is clear that towers were a component of the compounds of Eastern Han China. The tower was usually found in the northwestern corner of the estate and served, at the very least, as a watchtower[15]. Next to it was often found the armoury, well-stocked with weapons. The farmers and craftsmen on the estate often doubled as soldiers in this age when central government authority was waning and the individual manors in the countryside were the focus of local authority. The tower may have served also as a site for parties, with revelers gazing at the moon from the balconies as they listened to the gentle music of troupes of musicians.

Many questions remain to be answered. The most difficult are questions concerning the beliefs and intent of the people who made these objects. Nevertheless, it is possible to gain insights about these pottery towers by a careful examination of archaeology. Problems concerning the towers have been considered here within two contexts: the context of excavations throughout China and the context of one representative tomb. As has been demonstrated above, it is possible to determine that the towers in this exhibition are encompassed in the northern style, rather than the southern. They were made originally for tombs of the landed gentry of northern China. In addition, it is possible to state where and when the four towers in this exhibition were made: in an area in or near western Henan during the end of the Eastern Han dynasty (second century AD).

Tall Tower
Eastern Han.........Red earthenware with green glaze
ht: 144.8 cm

The Schloss Collection, New York. Photograph by Sarah Wells, courtesy of the Vassar College Art Gallery

H

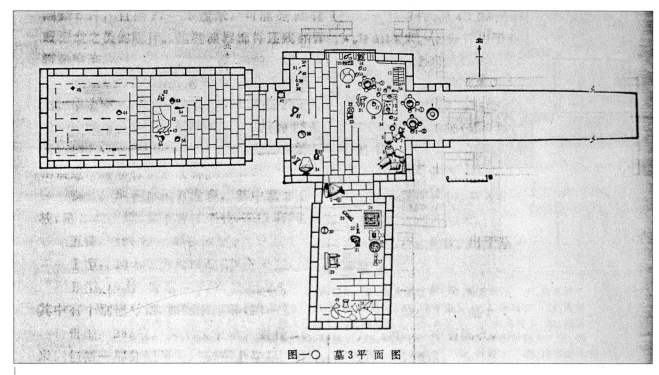

DIAGRAM OF TOMB 3 AT ZHANGWAN, Lingbao county, Henan excavated in 1973
From Wenwu, 1975, no. 11, p. 84

Tower found in 1954 at Jiunuzhong Village, Huaiyang County, Henan
Eastern Han........Red earthenware with remains of white slip and green glaze
ht: 144 cm

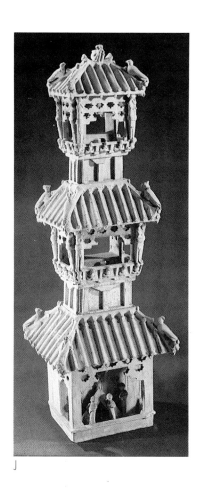

Notes

1. Burton Watson, Chinese Lyricism, Shih Poetry from the Second to the Twelfth Century, with translations, Columbia University Press, New York, 1971, p. 25.)
2. In Candace J. Lewis, "Tall Towers of the Han", Orientations, August, 1990, pp. 45–54, several questions about the pottery towers were addressed: When were they made? How were they made? Where were they made? What was the evolution from Western Han through the Eastern Han and into the early Six Dynasties periods?
3. Examples from Sichuan are not discussed in this essay. Several works are published, however, in Lucy Lim (organizer), Stories from China's Past, Han Dynasty Pictorial Tomb Reliefs and Archaeological Objects from Sichuan Province, People's Republic of China, 1987, colorplates 6 and 7, also plates 23 and 46. Both examples, one made of pottery and one of stone, are dated to the Eastern Han period. From Henan Provincial Museum, Henan Sheng Bowuguan, Zhongguo Bowuguan Cong Shu, vol. 7, Wenwu Press, 1982, no. 75
4. Guo Qinghua, "Shaanxi Mianxian Laodaosi Han mu" (A Han tomb at Laodaosi, Mian County, Shaanxi), Kaogu, 1985, no. 12, pp. 429–449 and Guo Qinghua, "Shaanxi Mianxian Laodaosi sihao Han mu fajue jianbao" (A brief report on the excavation of Han tomb no. 4 at Laodaosi, Mian County, Shaanxi), Kaogu yu wenwu, 1982, no. 2.
5. Zhang Guangzhong, "Xiangyang cutu Han luyou tao lou" (The Han dynasty green-glazed pottery tower unearthed at Xiangyang, Hubei), Wenwu, 1979, no. 2, p. 94.
6. George J. Lee, Selected Far Eastern Art in The Yale University Art Gallery, Yale University Press, New Haven and London, 1970, p. 71, no. 118.
7. Michele Pirazzoli-t'Serstevens, The Han Dynasty, p. 152. See also Terukazu Akiyama et al., Arts of China, Vol. I, Neolithic Cultures to the T'ang Dynasty, Kodansha International Ltd., Tokyo, Japan and Palo Alto, California, U.S.A., 1968, p. 176, nos. 321–322 and Wenwu, no. 11, 1959.

8. Cultural Relics Bureau of the Ministry of Culture and the Palace Museum (editors), Quan Guo Chutu Wenwu Zhenpin Chuan 1976–1984, pl. 29.
9. Cultural Relics Bureau of the Ministry of Culture and the Palace Museum (editors), Quan Guo Chutu Wenwu Zhenpin chuan 1976–1984 (A Selection of the Treasure of Archaeological Finds of the People's Republic of China 1976–1984), Wenwu Chubanshe, Beijing, 1985, no. 28. This tower was unearthed in Jinghai County, near Tianjin.
10. A similar example was excavated very recently in Hebei. See Wenwu, no. 1, 1990, pp. 19–30.
11. Henan Provincial Museum, Henan Sheng Bowuguan, Zhongguo Bowuguan Cong Shu, Vol. 7, Wenwu Chubanshe, 1982, no. 73. See also Wenwu, no. 2, 1974.
12. Henan Provincial Museum, Henan Sheng Bowuguan, Zhongguo Bowuguan Cong Shu, Vol. 7, Wenwu Chubanshe, 1982, no. 76.
13. Archaeological Work Team of the Yellow River Reservoir, "Yi jiu wu liu nian Henan Shanxian fajue jianbao" (A Report on the Excavations in Shanxian, Henan in 1956), Kaogu Tongxun, no. 4, 1957, pp. 1–9.
14. For a detailed discussion of this issue, see Wang Zhongshu, Han Civilization, Yale University Press, 1982, pp. 58–60.
15. Ibid., pp. 60–61.

Selected Bibliography

Akiyama, Terukazu et al., Arts of China, Vol. I, Neolithic Cultures to the T'ang Dynasty, Kodansha International Ltd., Tokyo, Japan and Palo Alto, California, U.S.A., 1968.

Dien, Albert E. et al., The Quest for Eternity, Chinese Ceramic Sculptures from The People's Republic of China, Los Angeles County Museum of Art, Chronicle Books, San Francisco, 1987.

Fontein, Jan and Wu Tung, Unearthing China's Past, Museum of Fine Arts, Boston, New York Graphic Society, Greenwich, Conn., 1973.

Lee, George J., Selected Far Eastern Art in The Yale University Art Gallery, Yale University Press, New Haven and London, 1970.

Lewis, Candace J., Into the Afterlife: Han and Six Dynasties Chinese Tomb Sculpture from the Schloss Collection, Vassar College Art Gallery, Poughkeepsie, N.Y., 1990.

Lewis, Candace J., "Tall Towers of the Han," Orientations, August, 1990, pp. 45–54.

Lim, Lucy (organizer), Stories from China's Past, Han Dynasty Pictorial Tomb Reliefs and Archaeological Objects from Sichuan Province, People's Republic of China, 1987.

Pirazzoli-t'Serstevens, Michele, The Han Dynasty, (translated by Janet Seligman), Rizzoli, New York, 1982.

Wang, Zhongshu, Han Civilization, (translated by K.C. Chang and Collaborators), Yale University Press, New Haven and London, 1982.

Watson, Burton, Chinese Lyricism, Shih Poetry form the Second to the Twelfth Century, with translations, Columbia University Press, New York, 1971.

Sources in Chinese

Cultural Relics Bureau of the Ministry of Culture and the Palace Museum (editors), Quan Guo Chutu Wenwu Zhenpin Chuan 1976— (A Selection of the Treasure of Archaeological Finds of the People's Republic of China 1976–1984), Wenwu Chubanshe, Beijing, 1985.

Guo Qinghua, "Shaanxi Mianxian Laodaosi Han mu" (A Han tomb at Laodaosi, Mian County, Shaanxi), Kaogu, 1985, no. 12, pp. 429–449.

Guo Qinghua, "Shaanxi Mianxian Laodaosi sihao Han mu fajue jianbao" (A brief report on the excavation of Han tomb no. 4 at Laodaosi, Mian County, Shaanxi), Kaogu yu wenwu, 1982, no. 2.

Henan Provincial Museum, Henan Sheng Bowuguan, Zhongguo Bowuguan Cong Shu, Vol. 7, Wenwu Chubanshe, 1982.

Kaogu, 1975, no. 2, pp. 116–134 (A brief report on the excavation of an Eastern Han tomb at Qilihe, Jianxi, Luoyang).

Kaogu Tongxun, 1956, no. 4, pp. 12–17 (A brief report of the cleaning up of an Eastern Han tomb at Dongshan, Guangzhou).

Wenwu, 1960, nos. 8–9, pp. 19–24 (The excavation of Han tomb no. 159 at Nanguan, Zhengzhou).

Wenwu, 1961, no. 1, pp. 56–66 (A brief account of the excavation of a group of Han dynasty tombs of the Yang family at Diaochao, Tongguan, Shaanxi).

Wenwu, 1972, no. 2, pp. 70–72 (A group of Han dynasty cultural relics unearthed in recent years in Wuzhou city, Guangxi Province).

Wenwu, 1974, no. 2, p. 70 (A painted pottery granary tower unearthed from an Eastern Han tomb in Jiaozuo, Henan).

Wenwu, 1975, no. 11, pp. 75–93 (The Han tombs at Lingbao, Zhangwan, Henan).

Zhang Guangzhong, "Xiangyang chutu Han luyou tao lou" (The Han dynasty green-glazed pottery tower unearthed at Xiangyang, Hubei), Wenwu, 1979, no. 2, p. 94.

CANDACE J. LEWIS

Is a Ph.D. candidate at the Institute of Fine Arts, New York University. The subject of her dissertation is "Pottery Towers of Han Dynasty China." She is the author of "Into the After-life: Han and Six Dynasties Chinese Tomb Sculpture from the Schloss Collection" (Vassar College Art Gallery, Poughkeepsie, New York 1990) and of "Tall Towers of The Han" Orientations, August 1990.

The Splendour of Han Pottery

by Chen Huasha
(Original in Chinese)

Various utensils were created by primitive man to meet his daily needs and for his survival. Pottery was his epoch-making creation, made by shaping clay and water into different forms, drying and firing them at certain temperatures so that they may harden into utensils. Since its creation, pottery-making had improved in technique through the dynasties of Shang, Zhou and Qin. More and more varieties of shapes, sizes and designs had been created not only as utensils for practical daily life, but also as ceremonial vessels and **mingqi** (明器), articles to be buried with the dead.

During the Western Han Dynasty, grey pottery was extensively produced and used throughout China. Many examples have been unearthed in recent times. The clay objects were dealt with differently and in accordance with the purpose for which they were intended. Some were mixed with coarse sand and some without; the temperature at which these were fired also varied, as did the content of iron oxide present in them. This resulted in different shades and varying degrees of hardness for the ware produced. Broadly speaking, plain pottery can be classified as grey pottery, red pottery, black pottery, grey pottery with a sandy body, and red pottery with a sandy body of varying hardness.

In line with social and economic advances, pottery-making had reached a new sophistication by the Han Dynasty. There were, not only painted pottery and glazed pottery, but also low-fired lead-glazed pottery which heralded the three-coloured glazed-ware (**sancai**) of the Tang Dynasty and other low-fired glazed-wares of the Ming and Qing. In addition there were high-fired greenwares.

Methods of Decoration

Among the decorative techniques of Han pottery, incising (划刻), stamping or impressing (压印), relief-moulding (模印浮雕), painting with pigments (涂色), and inscribing with vermilion were all used. Ridged designs — that is, bowstring lines or ridges in relief around the body of a vessel — were extensively used. These varied from bold to fine, were concave or convex, and complemented one another to produce striking decorative schemes. By the deft use of a knife, incised lines in linear, triangular, rippling or animalistic designs were created. Sometimes, concave grooves were carved between bold lateral lines — these resembled the tile lines engraved on Han jade. Stamping or impressing were used to imprint geometric, angular, rectangular and other motifs. Relief-moulding or embossing was done by luting the ornamentation on to the semi-dry vessel to obtain an effect of relief. After firing, the vessel could be painted with pigments or inscriptions in vermilion. Applying colours in this way produced vivid decoration, often equal in artistic merit to decorated Han lacquerware. However, these unfired colours were not permanent and wore off easily.

Decorative designs can be found on plain pottery, or they may be applied on as pigments, or glazed over.

Plain pottery, its inner and outer parts looking almost the same, may include grey, black and red pottery, grey being predominant. Lines, grooves, impressed inscriptions of dragons and other animals were simple designs appearing on such pottery.

Painted pottery was decorated by applying colour to the "plain" pottery in the same way as it was applied to lacquer, wood or bronze, that is, by blackening and applying powdered pigment, vermilion, ink or other colours. The lines were rich and vivid and came mostly from lacquerware designs. Colours used were red, brown, green, yellow, orange, ochre or blue, while calligraphy in the **li** (隸) or clerical script was mostly in vermilion.

In painted pottery a powdered pigment was applied to the vessel followed by coloured decoration either in linear designs or in imitation of designs found on bronzes. Designs were usually painted on. This was mostly done from the rim to the middle part of the vessel. The decorative motifs included the red dragon, tiger and sparrow, depicted separately or chasing one another amidst flowing clouds. Rippling and cloud lines might also be used, but all were colourful, bold and vivid. Sometimes, no powder background was applied, the colourful lines being directly painted onto the pottery vessel such as the **pen** (盆) or bowl unearthed from the tomb of Prince Liu Sheng in the Mancheng District of Hebei. The inner wall depicted white fishes chasing one another while the centre featured a snipe catching fish from the water, surrounded by vermilion lines — a lively and attractive decoration.

Glazed pottery refers particularly to the low-fired lead-glazed pottery. Glazes used were mainly derived from copper and iron with lead compounds such as flux. At about 700°C these melted into a brownish-yellow, green or orange-red glaze. This was a great step forward from plain pottery and an unsurpassed contribution of the Han Dynasty in pottery-making. Depending upon where these were produced, they could be classified as Northern glazed-ware or Southern glazed-ware.

Northern glazed-ware was first discovered in the Guanzhong District of Shaanxi, but until the time of Emperor Liu of Han, it was rarely found in the tombs at Xianyang and Xian. Lead-glazed pottery developed extensively only after the rule of Emperor Xuan of Han when it spread to the central plains.

Northern lead-glazed ware was mostly green, at times with a brownish-yellow glaze. Its decorative designs were mostly done by carving, relief-moulding or applique, and some had vermilion over the brownish-yellow glaze. As lead oxidizes easily, it reacted with moisture while buried to produce an iridescent effect, that is, the formation of a layer of glaze that looked like mica, uneven in thickness and looking very attractive. However, this phenomenon did not occur on vessels unearthed in more arid soil conditions.

Southern lead-glazed pottery was unearthed from tombs in great quantities, proving that by Eastern Han, lead-glazed pottery had spread from the north to the south over a wide region. Glazed pottery unearthed in Shaoxing, Zhejiang showed that this was mostly produced from kilns in Shangyu and Yongjia, and were hard and reddish in colour. Some had encircling lines around the body. Because of the presence of iron in the lead, the vessels looked greenish-brown. Also, only half the vessels were glazed. The surface was uneven and caused the glaze to appear patchy and glassy. Owing to these characteristics this ware is referred to as proto-greenware.

Han pottery produced in Guangdong had its own characteristics: its body was more porous and brittle, the glaze was thin and brownish-yellow in colour. Also, because of the wet climate, the glaze easily wore off.

Major categories of Han pottery

The art of Han pottery not only inherited the tradition of the past, but influenced what was to follow. Compared to the pottery of the Warring States and Pre-Qin periods, Han pottery art forms had evidently improved. As for the purpose Han pottery served, these could be broadly classified into four types: bronze-derived ceremonial vessels, utensils for daily life, vessels for burial purposes and architectural elements and building material.

Bronze-derived ceremonial vessels and pottery for daily use

During Western Han, bronze or copper coinage had been in great demand, however, as burial ceremonies evolved and changed, pottery had largely replaced bronze articles as burial vessels and daily utensils. Those that were most commonly used were :

1. The **fang** (钫), square or rectangular in shape, broad-based, with long legs and sometimes ears at both sides and had a cover.
2. The **pou** (瓿), jar or pot. Earlier ones were usually flat-mouthed, with sloping shoulders and either flat supporting legs or a flat base. Some had ears on the shoulder and flat oval covers with handles in the middle. Subsequently, during the Middle Western Han period, the shoulder became rounder, and the two ears level. The openings, mouth

SPLENDOUR OF HAN POTTERY

and supporting legs had disappeared. At a later stage, it grew bigger, became broad-mouthed, more globular with its two ears lower than the opening or mouth.

3. The **zhong** (钟) was broad-mouthed, long-necked with a round base, its body flat or with protruding decorations of bowstring lines, auspicious animals forms, wavy lines, etc and impressed inscriptions. It was also made with ears or bridging designs. Western Han vessels of this type were usually short and flat, but by the time of Eastern Han these had become elongated and rounded at the base. Most of these were excavated from Henan.

4. The **pan kou** (盘口壶) jar could reach a height of 80 cm like those unearthed in the Gaotang District of Shandong. It was made by applying low-fired lead glaze which gave it a greenish look of an even surface that was bright and shining as if new. Those from the Wei District were basically the same, but because of the dryness of the pit, there was little silver glaze. The shapes varied and the neck was either long and slender, or short and stubby, with bowstring lines, animals or wavy lines as designs on the surface.

5. The cocoon or egg-shaped **hu** (茧形壶) or jar was shaped like the cocoon of the silkworm or the duck egg placed horizontally, hence its name. The jar had a short neck and mouth with short, round supports at the base. Its body was impressed with bowstring lines or concave or convex lines like those appearing on Han jade. These lines were clear-cut. The cocoon-shaped jars varied in size and quality; the finer ones usually used as containers.

6. The duck-head **hu** (鸭首壶) or jar had its upper part looking like a duck's head; it had an opening on top, was long-necked with a flattened body and had a round base support (Fig. i).

7. The **xuantou kou ping** (蒜头口瓶) or garlic-mouth vessel looked like the duck-head jar, with a long neck, flat body, and round base support, the only difference being its mouth, which protrudes like the shape of garlic, hence, its name.

8. The **weng** (瓮) or pot had a large mouth or opening with a broad upper section, curving body and a flat base. It was usually undecorated.

9. The **guan** (罐) or jar. It usually had a broad upper section, a swollen middle portion, and a contracting lower part resting on a flat base.

10. The **zun** (樽) also known as **lian** (奁) was a goblet used at sacrificial ceremonies. It was known as **zun**, after the bronze goblet unearthed in Shanxi which bore the words in the **li** or clerical script: "one of two wine goblets crafted by Hu Fu of Zhongling, Weighing 24 katties, in the third year of Hoping (circa 28BC)". Henceforth, similar vessels came to be known as **zun**. It was usually short and straight, flat-based with three leg supports either curved or in the shape of a standing bear. Its body was plain with convex designs of clouds, auspicious animals, hunting scenes or bowstring lines. The lid had similar designs of clouds and animals. Some of these had the convex design of acrobats standing on their hands at the mouth of the vessel, a refreshing design.

Duck-head jar of grey pottery..........Western Han
(photo courtesy of Sotheby's)

11. The **ding** (鼎) or tripod was often seen in Han glazed-ware and was a continuation in the tradition of the Nine Tripods. This was usually used as a vessel to hold wine and meat. It had an open, broad mouth, an oval body. Flat-based with three supporting legs, it had two ears or handles attached to the middle body and a semi-circular cover with designs of sacrificial offerings of ox, sheep and hog or cloud and dragon or **boshan** (博山). Its evolution is best traced through its feet. Those created before the Western Han were plain while during the middle period, they had two eye-like motifs. Later these evolved into animal masks.
12. The **kui** (簋) was a vessel for holding food, broad-mouthed and with a rim, swollen body and rounded foot-rim. Its body usually had bowstring lines or designs in panels; and its lids impressed with auspicious animal designs.
13. The **jiao dou** (锥斗), shaped like the **xi** (洗), broad-bodied, with handles and three tall leg supports, a utensil to hold food.

Burial pottery and models

Han pottery inherited artistic Pre-Qin features and developed into an art of imbuing beauty in simple or crude form. It manifested the elegant, dignified and stately style of the period. Its development was consistent with other art forms of this period such as the murals, stone engravings and bronzeware. Human figures depicted the upper classes or common folk; all bore clean, simple but life-like images. Similarly for animal images. Some of the Han pottery works were for exhibition and decorative purposes, but most were used as **mingqi** or burial vessels, manifesting the elaborate funeral and burial traditions at the time.

Burial figures of pottery were varied and characteristic of the times too (Fig. ii-vii). The style was simple yet sincere. Deft skills showed the different social positions and occupations of the subjects, by various deportment, dress, appearance and features, etc. These pottery art forms, when studied together with other art treasures unearthed, present a vivid, realistic and colourful picture of Han society.

Human figures

Han pottery can be divided into human figures, animal and building models. In 1956, in Yangjiawan in Xianyang District of Shaanxi, about 2,500 pieces of colourful cavalry and infantry figurines were unearthed. These amply demonstrated the reality of the then social and military conditions. These figures also showed a continuing influence from the Pre-Qin period. The infantrymen stood erect and in formation, with different hairstyles painted in black or wearing hoods. Their armour, either in white or vermilion background, had breast-plates and back-plates in black, and they carried packs on their shoulders, all solemn and dignified (Fig. iii). Cavalrymen were fully equipped and mounted on horses, reaching a height of 68.5 cm (Fig. iv). Riders and horses were arranged differently. The horses, heads raised and tails sweeping upwards, were painted in white, black or red pigments. The back of these cavalrymen bore symbols. There were serial numbers on the buttocks of the horses.

Grey pottery figures in sitting position.........Western Han (photo courtesy of Sotheby's)

iii

Painted, glazed figure of an officer..........Western Han

iv

Painted and glazed cavalry figures..........Western Han

In May 1990, the tomb of Emperor Jing was discovered in the Zhengyang District of Wei Zheng. The burial figures in this tomb were arranged in strict formation (Fig. v). There were 24 narrow pits with figures arranged from east to west in 14 columns. The burial pits occupied a total area of 96,000 sq m. Each pit yielded more than 400 figures of painted pottery. These figures measured 62 cm each, and were without arms, but the sides of each shoulder had round holes penetrating the chest. They were all naked males. Their hair, beard, eyebrows and eyes were painted black while the entire body was in red. These figures were slender and well-proportioned, with proper facial features of varying expressions. All appeared in lively spirits. Judging from textile fragments or impressions, these naked figures were at first clothed. Compared with the Qin figures of this type and the Yangjiawan figures, these were more realistic and vivid especially with respect to dress.

In 1963 in a district in Sichuan some figures of musicians and performing artists were unearthed. These figures with their left hand holding up drums, their right the drum sticks, heads held high, body and knees bent, abdomen protruding, mouths open and tongues showing, were so vivid and life-like that they gave the impression of being in actual performance (Fig. vi)!

In 1987, in the Xingren District of Guizhou province, similar figures unearthed showed the performers seated with knees bent, with stringed instruments resting on their right knees. Their arms were raised and fingers crooked as if to strike

Brownish-green glazed dancing figures..........Western Han
(photo courtesy of Sotheby's)

Painted figures of vaudeville performers.........Western Han

ix

viii

Pit of burial figures discovered in Yangling.........Western Han

the chords, full of concentration on what they were doing (Fig. vii). The audience knelt at one side, their left hand raised, listening intently, and appearing enraptured.

In 1986, in Xuzhou, Jiangsu, the male protocol figurines unearthed were painted black on the head, the decoration on the right sleeves painted green, the cuffs in red, the collars edged in black. Their hands were tucked in their sleeves and they assumed a bowing posture. The detailed painted female figures had their official robes in white background, against which the fold of their robes were in black. They had neck scarves decorated red and wore long, flowing robes sweeping the ground. Their long hair and hair knots flowed down to the shoulder, and their eyes focussed straight ahead, in all solemnity and seriousness.

During the Han Dynasty vaudeville had become quite popular and had attained a high standard. In 1969, in Mt Wuying of Jinan in Shandong province, the vaudeville figures (Fig. viii) unearthed amply demonstrated the skills of these Chinese artistes 2000 years ago and the grand scale of such performances. Figures of the nobility stood on both sides of the stage to watch the performance of musicians and dancers. A figure stood on a plate while others performed calisthenics. These were vivid and lively. Additionally, other figures unearthed also showed, either individually or in groups, musicians performing wind and string instruments or beating drums. They were all depicted realistically and convincingly (Fig. ix). There were also vessels depicting men in acrobatic posture or riders on horseback, in captivating performance.

In 1990, the Archaeological Division of the Chinese Institute of Science discovered for the first time, south of Xiangjia Gang village in the Liucunbao district of Xian, sites of official kilns of the Western Han thought to be used for the production of pottery figures. Twenty-one such kilns in three groups, arranged in triangular formation, were uncovered. Each kiln had an ante-room, a firing compartment, kiln bed and a smoke tunnel. Between the kiln bed and firing compartment were brick partitions with inlets between bricks to admit fire and heat. Artefacts unearthed from these kilns numbered thousands. Besides moulds and utensils used in the production of pottery, most were naked figures of similar build: bare upper body, without arms, height 50-60 cm and of both sexes, but mainly males. Their facial expressions were varied. According to the Debates on Salt and Iron, (盐铁记) it was a Han practice to dress the carved figures (for burial with the dead) in light, glossy silk. Hence the nude figures must have been dressed differently in accordance with their standing.

In two of the kilns, 350 to 400 unfired clay figures were found. These were arranged in an orderly way.

These nude figures were similar to those unearthed from the tombs of Emperor Xuan of Han, Emperor Jing, Emperor Wu and Emperor Zhao. Hence, it could be deduced that the kilns unearthed were official production sites of **mingqi** or pottery burial objects for the imperial household, administered by a specific palace department in charge of such production.

SPLENDOUR OF HAN POTTERY

*Groom leading a brownish-green glazed horse..........Eastern Han
(photo courtesy of T. T. Tsui Museum of Art)*

*Painted winged dragon..........Western Han
(photo courtesy of T. T. Tsui Museum of Art)*

Animal forms

Animal art forms of the Western Han were very lively and realistic. They also had special features, for example, the three-horned beast with its tail curled upwards similar to the rhinocerous. The Chinese unicorn and dragon, vigorous and powerful; the ox, horse and goat, reclining or standing, fat and well-fed, domestic fowl like the duck and hen, were all vigorous and full of life.

Among the most vivid and attractive of other Han animals was the horse. All horses were in the equine style of **Da wan** (大宛) or Ferghana, fat and strong, powerfully-built but with slender limbs. These were either plain, in white slip or vermilion-coated (Fig. 38), painted with other pigments or lead-glazed in decorative designs. Some were with riders and others without, but most were with saddles and bridles.

In January 1991, the pottery horses of Eastern Han exhibited at the T. T. Tsui Museum of Art, (香港徐氏艺术馆) Hongkong, were masterpieces in this category (Fig. x). The horses showed the man leading the horse with raised arms, reins tightened, with kicking hoofs and raised tails, neighing with its head slanted and panting through the nostrils.

Judging from these cavalry horses, the cavalrymen must have been in orderly and awe-inspiring formation behind the horses. Besides these, the exhibits of dragons (Fig. xi) and bullock carts (Fig. xii) by the same gallery were also rarities. These were all unearthed in Sichuan. The dragon with a posed head, protruding chest, eyeing skywards, firm front limbs with rear limbs arched, and wings painted at

*Bullock cart in grey pottery..........Western Han
(photo courtesy of T. T. Tsui Museum of Art)*

the shoulders, looked as if, at any moment, it would ride the clouds and ascend into heaven with great poise and dignity. The bullock cart was in contrast; the bullock straining to pull the cart, against the unhurried manner of the passengers, who were shown with hands folded into their sleeves.

Domestic fowl and beasts were often shown in huts or cages. For example, figures unearthed in Sanmenxia looked like houses, and goats were shown sleeping or resting in them. The pig-sty was circular, with booths around its fence, and a fat, sturdy mother pig can be seen reclining within the fence, suckling her piglings. From Changsha, the hen-house unearthed resembled a house with hens and cockerels fighting to peck at their food. The dog was depicted in more ways than one, creating images that also varied greatly (Fig. 154, 155, 158). There were strong and sturdy ones, and also thin and slender ones, the longest measuring 90 cm in length. Those with long, slender limbs and small waists looked like the Alsatian, with decorative designs of ribbons around the neck. Some were shown standing, others on all fours, yet others appeared to be listening intently or, with raised heads, barking fiercely and looking very aggressive.

The potters were adept in capturing the expressive features of the animal and at creating life-like and realistic art forms.

Models of buildings

Models of castles and dwellings of Han gentry had also been unearthed (Fig. xiii, xiv, xv and Fig. 192). One of those unearthed from a Han tomb in the Wanfu District of Hebei showed a three-tier structure, with female figures included in them. Another model from the Shen District of Henan was also a three-tier pavilion standing in a circular pond with water-fowl swimming in the pond. Around the pond guards were on patrol, while others guard with bows and arrows. Inside the pavilion, officials or scholars were having games of chess or other competitive entertainment. As for the four-tiered model unearthed from the Gaotang district of Shandong Province, the structure was magnificent and grandoise. Due to the low-humidity of Shandong, the pottery models unearthed all showed glossy and glazed surfaces, appearing new because of the lack of lead reaction.

Such models varied greatly in height, with the highest reaching ten storeys, while the ponds depicted were either square, rectangular or circular, but each with specific features. Some of these models had oxidized silver glaze, making the pottery glossy and transparent rather like crystal.

vi

Story-teller in grey pottery.........Eastern Han

vii

Flautist in grey pottery.........Eastern Han

Lamps

Another aspect of Han pottery was the variety of lamps. They generally showed a supporting base and a pillar structure above it, with **boshan** lamp covers. The larger ones usually had three-section pillars rising from the base while branches stretched out from the different sections terminating in dishes containing fuel or oil to light the lamps. Others were in a bird design with outspread wings. The handles were intricately designed and elaborate, of which the **jiulian deng** (九莲灯) or Nine-Lotus Lamp stood out most conspicuously. In addition, there were lamps which depicted male figures holding cylindrical containers on their heads (Fig. 180) or with outstretched arms, the containers holding fuel or oil to light the lamp. Other lamps showed female figures breast-feeding babies (Fig. 181). There were also lamps in the form of three bowls joined together, with two handles attached. (Fig. 150).

Stoves

The pottery stove varied in size, but was usually elongated, with one end rounded and the other straight, and an opening to the fire-chamber. The stove had three, four or five openings on top and on it were placed utensils such as the **fu** (釜) or **zeng** (甑). The edge of the stove was either plain or decorated with moulded designs of utensils such as the fork, knife or of fish and meat, meant to convey wishes for an abundant after-life. There were also rectangular stoves and spectacular tortoise-shaped stoves with long necks, with their heads as chimney outlets and four legs at the base.

Granaries

Another type of **mingqi** model was the granary or **kun** (囷) in various styles (Fig. 117, 118 and Fig. xvi). This was first discovered in Qin tombs, but had become a popular practice by the time of Emperor Wu of Han. During the initial stage of Western Han, these granary models had round mouths, circular bodies, flat bases and covers in the shape of an inverted bowl. By Middle Western Han, the supports had turned circular and three leg supports were added to the flat base. By Eastern Han, the lower portion had contracted so that the upper body was broader and the three supporting legs were done away with, leaving the model with a flat base, as before. From the Baoji District of Shaanxi, models with a cylindrical body, ears at the top and three supporting legs at the base had been unearthed. Purple

Tower in grey pottery..........Eastern Han

xiii

Pottery model of a manor-house in brown glaze.........Eastern Han

xiv

*Green glazed model of a house..........Eastern Han
(photo courtesy of Sotheby's)*

lines and other decorative designs were painted over the brownish-ochre glaze. From Rongyang in Henan was unearthed pottery granary models with high walls. Swirling clouds in black were painted on the white background thus creating a very mysterious atmosphere. Similar articles unearthed from Luoyang were mostly cylindrical, round-mouthed, flat-based with three bear feet as supports. Covers were shaped like inverted bowls. The body was decorated by three to four groups of bowstring designs and words in vermilion were written in the clerical script, for example, "ten thousand piculs (   ) of wheat", and "corn and millet of ten thousand piculs". There was one such model with words written in the 4th year of Chuping (circa AD190) by one Wang. This was a precious piece as the year and the name of the potter had been identified.

Pottery as architectural elements and building material

The palace of Qin and Han were magnificent and grand. The A-Fang Palace of Qin and the Weiyang and Jianzhang Palace of Han were outstanding and glorious in the history of Chinese architecture. But with the passing of time, the ravages of war and natural forces, they were brought to ruin. But from what was left in the form of Qin bricks and Han tiles, we are still able to catch a glimpse of the rich and magnificent art of building during these periods.

Tiles and murals

The Han eaves tile ends were mostly circular (Fig. 5,6). Tiles of coarse sand unearthed from old Changan were invaluable for the study of ancient architecture. Some scholars and poets had even converted these into ink-stones for their use. Han tiles were usually impressed with words in the seal script such as **Han bing tian xia** (汉并天下) or Han united the kingdom, **Shang-lin** (上林), **Chang sheng wu ji** (畏生无极) or everlasting life, **Yong tai wu jiang** (永泰无疆) peace without limit, etc, while others were decorated with designs of auspicious clouds, dragon, tiger or the **Xuan-wu** (玄武女神) goddess. The tiles unearthed from the bed-chamber tomb of Emperor Wu of Han bore these twelve words: " 与民世世，天地相方，永安年正 " or Forever with the people, everlasting with heaven and earth and justice and peace unlimited. Others also bore auspicious words. In 1955, in Baotou of Inner Mongolia, tiles bearing the words, Shan yu tian jiang (单于天降) heaven-descended Khan, were unearthed. Together with those found in the Jianzhang Palace site of Changan, they were highly valued as objects of study and aesthetic appreciation.

The Han rulers advocated filial piety and the dead were usually buried with great pomp and ceremony. They also believed that the dead should be served just

Brown glazed quintuple grain jar..........Eastern Han

as the living. Hence nobility and the rich had elaborate tombs built for them. These were replicas of mansions in which they lived when alive, except that the burial chambers were lined with large quantities of models of precious articles and items they had enjoyed in life. Besides the burial paraphernalia, pictorial tiles were also used to decorate the walls of the burial chambers. Some even had mural paintings on the walls.

Pictorial tiles and stones with distinctive features had been unearthed in many provinces. Those found in the north of Shandong and Jiangsu had fully designed surfaces. Often a tile or stone was sub-divided into bands, each with a subject of its own. However, those found in Nanyang of Henan were not sub-divided into panels or bands. Each tile or stone had a unique theme of its own. Those found in Shanxi were a mixture of both categories.

Han pictorial tiles were varied and colourful, most of which depicted chariot processions (Fig. 12), feasting and acrobatic performance, farming and harvesting, mythological or historical stories and legends. The **kongxin zhuan** (空心砖) or hollow bricks of Western Han, unearthed in Liantong in Shanxi, had pictorial designs of robed figures holding shields, with dragon, phoenix, birds and animals designs. On square, solid bricks, geometrical designs had been found. The long bricks had the words **Wei Yang** (未央), longevity (延年益寿), shining evermore with the sun and the moon (兴天相传，日月同光) and moulded inscriptions.

Yet another type of pictorial tile was unearthed in 1990, at Xichang in Sichuan. Known as the **you wei pu** (有尾仆), it is shaped like the trapezium, 57 cm in height, with the lower part in light relief of dragons and other figures. The figures were usually nude females, with well-shaped limbs, their ribs barely showing while, at the middle of their buttocks, tails of 4 cm could be discerned. These females wore head-dresses and were vividly dancing with balls in their hands. The edge of these tiles had border designs of dragons, tiger, the three-egged crow, the lotus and various geometric lines. Xichang, known as Gongdu in ancient times, was the main district in which the **pu** (仆夷) barbarians lived, and the discovery of these trapezium tiles provided new insights into the life of the ancient tribes.

Wells

Han architecture also included the practical, underground wells constructed of pottery blocks. Those found in Beijing were mostly discovered in the Xuanwu Gate district. They usually had a diameter of about 150 cm. Curved, sectional walls were joined piece by piece with the top part being broader, and gradually narrowing downwards. The walls of these wells had circular holes to allow underground water to flow into the well. From the models unearthed amongst the **mingqi** or burial vessels, it could be seen that these were usually cylindrical or rectangular-shaped. The well supports, the well shelter, the pulleys, the rope and the water bucket proved valuable for research on Han architecture. The wooden instruments or utensils used at the mouth of the well had long disappeared.

(Figures in The Catalogue are referred to in this article).

Acknowledgement

The writer wishes to record her sincere thanks to her teacher, ceramics specialist, appraiser and Research Fellow from the National Palace Museum, Mr Geng Baochang (耿宝昌), for his encouragement and advice.

CHEN HUASHA (陈华莎)

Researcher, Chinese Cultural Relics Bureau, Beijing.

THE CATALOGUE

Classified and dated by
LU YAW

Written by
ENG-LEE SEOK CHEE
KENSON KWOK
JOHN MIKSIC
LISE YOUNG LAI

Plain Pottery

2

3

2. Cocoon
Qin or Early Western Han..........Grey earthenware
ht: 39 cm, length: 46 cm, width: 30 cm, dia (mouth): 15.3 cm

The burnished black body bears traces of red, green, and blue pigments. The only other decoration consists of eight sets of double incised lines encircling the body vertically.

3. Cocoon
Qin or Early Western Han..........Grey earthenware
ht: 40 cm, length: 43 cm

The only decoration consists of twelve vertical bands of triple incised grooves, two ridges around the neck, and incised circles at the extremities of the vessel.

1. Covered Fumigation Stem Bowl →
Warring States or Early Han..........Grey earthenware
ht: 21 cm, dia: 16 cm

The body has a horizontal band of rectangles crossed by carved diagonal lines. The lid has three bands of identical decoration, the uppermost carved deeply enough to perforate the clay. The lid has a slightly flaring hollow knob with a series of circular perforations around its lower portion, and three smoke emission slits separated by cross-hatched design. There are possible traces of a white slip. The object has a high footring with incised triangles.

4. Stove
Warring States or Early Han..........Grey earthenware
(Base) ht: 11 cm, length: 24 cm, width: 17.5 cm
(Pot) ht: 8.5 cm, dia: 17 cm

*The stove is in the shape of a rectangular box with a square opening; the top surface has a large circular hole for the detachable cooking pot, and a smaller hole towards the back, perhaps to serve as the flue. The pot is rounded below like a bowl, while its upper portion narrows to a short straight neck. The outer surface of the stove is impressed all over with cord markings, common in Han pottery.
The base is completely open, and cut flat.*

4

5   6

5. **Eaves Tile End**
Western Han..........Grey earthenware
dia: 15.5 cm, thickness: 2.5 cm

*The half-round, vault-shaped body of the eaves tile has broken off. A central boss in relief is encircled by two raised strings, around which are arranged the four seal script characters **yu hua wu ji** in relief (possibly meaning - everlasting splendour). The whole is encircled by a further raised string and a broad, flat rim.*
Such eaves tile ends are usually associated with Western Han palace sites.

8. **Pillar**
Western Han..........Grey earthenware
(Pillar) ht: 79 cm
(Capital) width: 25 cm, depth: 18 cm

The shaft of the pillar, which has a chamfered edge at its mid-section, sits on a plinth. The capital on top has a similar shape to the plinth below. The decoration on the sides of the pillar consists of friezes or borders made by the repeated application of stamp moulds. One stamp depicts two crested dragons, the one behind biting the tail of the one in front. The other stamp produces a simple grooved pattern, which is used as a border to divide some of the dragon friezes.
The fourth side of the pillar is randomly stamped. The top surface of the capital is similarly roughened.

6. **Eaves Tile End**
Western Han..........Grey earthenware
dia: 17 cm, thickness: 3 cm

*The end of this eaves tile is decorated with a central boss and raised strings dividing the circular field into four quadrants. Arranged within are the four seal script characters **chang sheng wu ji** (life everlasting) in relief.*

8

7. **Pillar Capital** →
Western Han..........Grey earthenware
ht: 55.2 cm, width: 19.4 cm, depth: 20.5 cm

This anthropomorphic capital shows a seated figure grasping what is intended to be an extension of the pillar proper. Its large head is expressively moulded and decorated with incised lines to represent eyebrows, bulging eyes, slightly protuberant cheekbones, nose, ears, and a grinning, bearded mouth.
The sides of the figure and other areas of the capital are decorated with friezes created by the repeated use of stamp moulds. At least four different stamps have been used. One depicts a hunting scene in which a mounted bowman rides at full gallop through a rocky landscape, turning round to take aim at a tiger. This stamp may be seen on the sides of the figure and in the upper part of the pillar extension. Parts of another stamp with tree and rock motifs are also visible at either end of the uppermost horizontal frieze. Some of the stamps have been applied upside down.
The vertical friezes on the pillar extension consist of a central column of double dragon stamps which is bracketed on either side by friezes with typical trellis design.
Similar anthropomorphic capitals on columns are known to exist in pairs, suggesting a symmetrical placement at some key point in a tomb, such as for example on either side of an entrance.

Plain Pottery

9. Pillar

Western Han..........Grey earthenware
(Pillar) ht: 109 cm
(Capital) width: 17 cm, depth: 17.5 cm

Similar in overall design to fig.8, although with a less prominent capital and plinth, this pillar is decorated with at least four different stamps.

Horizontal friezes of decoration made up of stamps of various designs – peacocks, fish amongst swirling water, and a grooved pattern – are impressed on the capital. The same stamps, together with an additional one of a hunting scene with mounted bowman pursuing a tiger, are used to create vertical friezes on the shaft of the pillar. The chamfered edges of the shaft are also stamped. Details of decoration on the plinth are no longer legible.

10. Pillar

Western Han..........Grey earthenware
ht: 97.5 cm, width: 24 cm, depth: 16.5 cm

The nib-like flanges on either side of this pillar suggest that it is a vertical element in the walls of the tomb chamber, interlocking with other vertical or horizontal members, rather than a semi-free standing architectural element like fig.8 or fig.9.

Six different stamps are used in the decoration of the front and back surfaces. A central column of motifs is enclosed by two long scored lines. In the middle are six diamonds containing small bosses in relief arranged around a larger, central boss. Small florets are separately stamped on either side. Above and below are three different figurative motifs, crisply defined within their rectangular or square fields.

The middle stamps depict a two-storey pavilion with tile roofs and what appear to be balconies on each floor with railings and lattice-work panels. In the foreground, two confronting human figures prepare to launch their arrows into the air.

*A mounted bowman is the feature of the innermost stamps, with a bird in flight, perhaps meant to be his target, also shown. Rockwork representing a wild landscape is indicated below the horse's stomach. Around two sides of the square is an inscription which includes the characters **ba qian li** (eight thousand **li**).*

Plain Pottery

11. Wall Tile

Eastern Han..........Grey earthenware
ht: 25 cm, width: 41 cm, thickness: 5 cm

A lively scene is depicted on this relief moulded tile. A rider is seated on his frisky mount, a mythical deer with antlers and small wings on its front and rear flanks. A figure, possibly that of an attendant or groom, holds out in one hand what appears to be a pouch.

11

12

12. Wall Tile

Eastern Han..........Grey earthenware
length: 34 cm, width: 17 cm, thickness: 3 cm

Part of a procession is depicted on this moulded tile. A prancing horse draws a chariot with a flat, canopied top which shelters a driver and passenger. Two attendants dressed in tunic, trousers and hooded headgear precede the horse on foot. The moulding has a flat rather than a rounded surface.

13. Manservant

Eastern Han..........Grey earthenware
ht: 41.5 cm

The figure probably represents one of the army of menials on a Han estate. He is weighed down by a container or bucket in each hand. His headgear is formed of two crossed flaps of material and his long robe is belted at the waist. The body of the figure is hollow.

14. Dancer

Eastern Han..........Grey earthenware
ht: 50 cm

Depicted in a stately posture, this dancer is attired in a high headgear and a long wide-sleeved gown, girdled at the waist. This type of pottery figure is commonly found in Sichuan Province tombs.

13

14

Plain Pottery

Painted Pottery

16. *Cocoon*
Western Han..........Grey earthenware with vermilion, red, white and green pigments
ht: 28 cm, length: 30 cm

The elaborate painted design consists of three vertical vermilion bands bordered in white and decorated with criss-crossed lines. The space between the bands contains scrolls in red, green, and white, with white dots. The two ends of the cocoon are decorated by a circle containing a spiral.

17. *Cocoon*
Western Han..........Grey earthenware with traces of pink, red, cream, white and black pigments
ht: 27 cm, length: 33 cm, dia (mouth): 9.9 cm

Pink, red, cream, white, and black pigments form three vertical bands separated by red stripes. The motifs include zigzags, geometric patterns and straight lines between bands of swirling scrolls. At each end is a red spiral edged in white. The flange is painted in lines of alternating bands of colour inside the mouth.

16

17

15

15. *Cocoon*
Western Han..........*Grey earthenware with vermilion, dark red and white pigments*
ht: 28 cm, length: 33 cm, dia: 23 cm

The richly painted ornamentation consists of vermilion scrolls on the rim, and three symmetrically arranged dark red bands dividing the body into four panels. The two central panels contain white scrolls. The two panels at the extremities bear a circular "eye" motif.

18. **Vase**
Western Han..........*Grey earthenware with traces of red and white pigments*
ht: 29.3 cm, width: 18.6 cm, dia (mouth interior): 9 cm

*The object, imitating an archaic bronze vessel in form, bears two **taotie** masks in detailed relief applied on two sides; they have no rings. There are traces of red and white painted designs of scrolls and triangles.*

19. **Wine Jar**
Western Han..........*Grey earthenware with red and white pigments*
ht: 22.5 cm, width: 23.5 cm, dia (mouth): 7 cm

Painted red and white stripes decorate the base. It would seem that the upper part of the body had a semi-circular outline in red and white enclosing a red curvilinear motif. The shoulders bear circular patterns. Red and white stripes encircle the neck. The object rests on a high hollow rectangular foot.

Painted Pottery

20, 21, 22 & 23. **Hu**
Western Han..........*Grey earthenware with pigments which include white, vermilion, blue, red and lavender*
20. ht: 56 cm, dia (max.): 36 cm, dia (mouth): 19 cm
21. ht (with lid): 51 cm, dia: 33 cm, dia (mouth): 16 cm
22. ht: 32 cm, dia: 22.5 cm
23. ht: 29.5 cm, dia: 23.8 cm, dia (mouth): 10 cm

Three of these four **hu** *(fig.20, 21 and 22) are decorated with moulded* **taotie** *masks. In the case of fig.20 and 21, the masks are enclosed within two parallel border lines circling the mid-bodies while on fig.22 the masks are appliqued on the shoulder.*

As is usually the case, the painted decoration on these **hu** *is enclosed within sets of parallel lines: spirals, scrolls, geometric patterns and abstract motifs are painted in a variety of colours including white, vermilion, blue, red and lavender. Fig.21 and 22 have a dark-brown to black slip which offsets the pigments most effectively. Fig.22 is especially outstanding, with its fairly well preserved decorations reminiscent of bronze inlay work.*

20

21

23

22

Painted Pottery

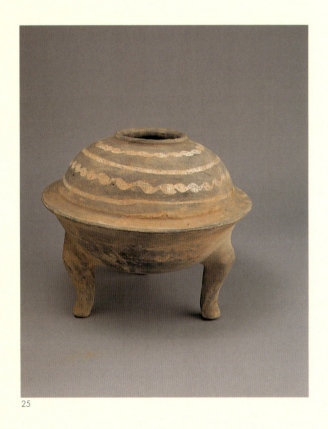

25

24 & 25. **Ding**   *26.* **Tripod**
Western Han..........Grey earthenware with various pigments including white, beige, red, black and yellow
24. ht: 10 cm, dia: 19.5 cm
25. ht: 16.2 cm, dia: 20 cm, dia (mouth): 5.3 cm
26. ht: 7.2 cm, dia: 19 cm, dia (mouth): 5.3 cm

In fig.24, three scrolls painted in red, white and light beige decorate the top of the lid. Painted bands decorate the edge of the lid as well as the body.
Fig.25 and 26 each have a painted flange around their midpoint and vaguely zoomorphic feet. White dominates in the decoration of fig.25 while the scroll motif on fig.26 is in red and black with a yellow background. Two moulded ox-like heads with horns and nose rings have been applied to the body of fig.26.

24

26

Painted Pottery

27. **Tripod**
Western Han..........*Grey earthenware with red and white pigments*
ht: 12 cm, dia: 17.5 cm, dia (mouth): 3.5 cm

The cover is shaped like an upturned bowl with a high footrim and rests on a lipped flange moulded around the vessel. Ornamented with red and white bands, the lid is pierced with three holes at the top, in the area enclosed by the "footrim". The vessel is decorated with leaf scrolls in red and white within painted bands. The holes on the lid and the raising of the vessel by three animal feet suggest that it may have served as an incense burner or a steamer.

27

28. **Tripod**
Western Han..........*Grey earthenware with red pigment*
ht (body without lid): 10 cm, ht (lid): 5.5 cm
ht (body and lid): 13 cm
dia (body): 18.5 cm, dia (mouth): 4.1 cm, dia (lid): 18 cm

Traces of red pigment on the lid form horizontal stripes at the lower edge, and indistinct motifs enclosed within a central band. The flat top is demarcated by a ridge and encloses a painted abstract design. The body has a medial flange, decorated on its upper surface with a wavy stripe. Above the flange the body bears a painted panel with indistinct motifs surmounted by three horizontal stripes. The tripod stands on three simple, graceful pediform feet.

28

Painted Pottery

29.

29. Owl-shaped Container
Western Han..........Grey earthenware with white, ochre, black and red pigments
ht: 28 cm

White pigment mainly, with some ochre, black and red, delineate the bird's eyes, eyebrows, feathers and wings.
The owl's beak, "ears" and especially-large, clumsy-looking feet are moulded, the outsized feet providing greater stability to the container. The bird's head is turned ninety degrees to the left and the raised rim at the top implies that it was originally fitted with a lid.
The purpose of this type of container remains obscure; however, it has been suggested that it could have been for wine or medicine.

30. Owl-shaped Container ➤
Western Han..........Grey earthenware with grey slip and white, ochre and black pigments
ht: 16.5 cm

A light-grey slip covers the darker grey body of the bird, though not its head, and white, ochre and black pigments simulate eyes, feathers and wings.
In addition to a moulded beak, the bird has two simply moulded legs on either side of its stout body which give it the appearance of sitting on its rump.
The owl's head serves as lid and has a two-centimeter flange on its underside which slots into the body.

32. **Female Attendant**
Western Han..........Light-grey earthenware painted with white, black, dark red and vermilion pigments
ht: 73.5 cm

This female attendant is modelled with two holes where her folded hands meet. Her white painted face has delicately indicated features, adding to the overall impression of restrained elegance.
The figure is moulded in two longitudinal sections and there is an oval hole in the back; the head is detachable.

Painted Pottery

33. **Female Attendant**
Western Han..........Grey earthenware with red, white and black pigments
ht: 68 cm

Modelled in simplified volumes, the figure affects the usual frontal pose, but in this case, the arms are not held out in front of the body. The two holes cut into the sleeves were originally intended for the insertion of detachable hands, which probably held an offering. The attendant has the conventional hairstyle with a centre parting, and wears the typical long-sleeved wrap-over outer robe. The V-shaped opening reveals a glimpse of the top of a white inner garment which covers the neck. The detachable head of the figure fits into a hole at the top of the moulded hollow body.

33

31

31. **Female Attendant**
Western Han..........Grey earthenware with white, black, brown and red pigments
ht: 73 cm

Wearing a typical long sweeping robe, this female attendant stands with head bent in a deferential pose that also conveys a quiet dignity. Her hands are hidden in the folds of her wide sleeves, where two holes cut at an angle suggest that she had originally carried a staff or similar object. Dressed in the characteristic manner of Western Han women, her hair is parted in the centre and pulled away from the face into a low bun at the back. The figure has a detachable head. It is moulded with a hollow interior and a slit at the back.

Painted Pottery

34

34. **Kneeling Servant**
Western Han..........Grey earthenware with red, white and black pigments
ht: 17.5 cm

Depicted in a frontal pose, this servant figure is kneeling with slightly bent head and hands clasped together in front. The figure, which has been made in a two-piece longitudinal mould is hollow at the base. It is attired in the usual red-bordered loose robe with wide sleeves. The hair is painted black and tied in a topknot.

35. **Kneeling Servant**
Western Han..........Grey earthenware with white, black and red pigments
ht: 16.8 cm

Depicted in a kneeling position with her hands held in front of her, the figure wears a loose wrap-around robe with long wide sleeves, bordered in red at the edge of the collar and sleeves. Traces of white pigment remain on the faintly smiling face. Her hair is pulled back and dressed in a long bun at the back; the tip of the bun is partly visible from the front.
The seams of the two-piece mould can be seen along the sides of the figure.

35

Painted Pottery

36.

36. **Horse**
Western Han..........Grey earthenware with red slip and vermilion and white pigments
ht: 38 cm, length: 39.7 cm

The animal is covered in white slip and then painted uniformly in an earthy red colour. A bridle has been added in vermilion with white decorative dots and there are medallions on the cheeks, muzzle and forehead.
The horse has a finely formed mane and a clipped forelock. Bulging eyes, flaring nostrils and a partially open mouth give it a lively expression. The strength of the animal is conveyed by its broad neck and body and powerful buttocks and legs.
The various parts of the horse have been moulded separately and then luted together, except for the knotted tail and missing ears which are detachable.

Painted Pottery

38

39

38. Horse
Western Han..........Grey earthenware with red slip and white, vermilion, orange, pale blue and pale green pigments
ht: 35.2 cm, length: 40 cm

This horse with a detachable head is painted in deep red. A bridle seemingly fastened by metal medallions has been painted in white; nostrils, eyes and mouth are in red. A white, orange and blue ribbon swirls around the neck.
The body is painted with a highly decorative harness in orange and white scrolls and bands, accentuated with green dots. Green, blue, orange and white swirling ribbons appear on the right-hand side of the body only and on the horse's breast.
The base of the body is painted and has four holes for the missing legs.

39. Horse
Western Han..........Buff earthenware with red slip and white and black pigments
ht: 35.5 cm, length: 48.5 cm

Remains of a red slip can be observed on this horse with a detachable head. The eyes have been detailed with black and white pigments and there are traces of a white bridle.
The head has been sculpted with a flat implement which gives it an angular appearance while the hollow body has been moulded.
Four holes are found on the underbody, for the missing legs.

Painted Pottery

42.

42. Pair of single-horned Mythical Beasts
Late Eastern Han or later..........Grey earthenware with white slip and traces of red pigments
ht: 13.5 cm, length: 22 cm

This pair of mythical beasts are replicas of bronze weights used to hold down the edges of seating mats.
The single "horn" along the back of each animal's head is in the shape of a long, narrow projection, with a scalloped outer edge.
Other moulded details include thick eyebrows, whiskers and mane, bulbous eyes, snub nose, well defined rump, and tail curling under the body.
Each animal is coiled around a cylindrical opening whose specific function has not been clearly established.
Traces of red pigment are visible around the teeth and mouth.

Painted Pottery

37. **Horse**
Western Han..........Grey earthenware with white slip and red pigment
ht: 60 cm, length: 54 cm

The horse's body is covered in white slip with red pigment discernible only inside one of its flaring nostrils.
Accurately made, it reflects the realistic animal style adopted by the Han potter.

40. **Head of a Horse**
Western Han...........Grey earthenware with red, white, lavender and black pigments
ht: 29 cm

This painted head shows a red background colour against which are painted white teeth outlined in black ink and a harness in lavender and white. Red, black and white pigments are swirled around the neck. The moulded head is hollow.

Painted Pottery

41.

41. *Horse and Rider*
Western Han..........Grey earthenware with white slip and brown, lavender, black and red pigments
ht: 25.5 cm, length: 26.5 cm

The body is covered in white slip, with the harness picked in dark brown. Ribbons and bridle fittings are painted in lavender and streamers extending from the chest towards the back are red. The animal's teeth are outlined in black. Other painted linear patterns have become indistinct.
Perforations on top of the head are meant to hold the missing ears and a hole in the middle of the saddle retains the rider in place. Four holes of approximately one millimeter each on the horse's underside are for the missing legs.

Painted Pottery

44

44. Ox and Cart
Eastern Han or later..........*Orange-pink earthenware with white, red, black and reddish-brown pigments*
(Ox) ht: 8.5 cm, length: 18.3 cm
(Cart) ht: 26 cm, length: 20.3 cm, dia (wheels): 16.5 cm

45. Ox and Cart
Eastern Han or later..........*Grey earthenware with white slip and black pigment*
ht. of cart: 25.5 cm, length of ensemble: 47.5 cm

These two exhibits illustrate the commoner's mode of transportation in Han times.
The painted decoration of the cart in fig. 44 supplements extensive relief detail to provide a delightful representation of what would seem to be a rather fanciful cart.

45

Painted Pottery

43. **Winged Dragon**
Late Eastern Han or later..........Grey earthenware with white slip
length: 31 cm

This highly stylized dragon is in the shape of an S with an added appendage forming an elongated tail. The slight, reptilian figure displays two well-formed wings, two vestigial front legs and two complete hind legs.
In addition to a patchy white slip, a decoration in reserve can be observed on the inside of one of the wings.

Painted Pottery

50

46

46, 47, 48, 49 & 50. **Farm Animals**
Eastern Han..........Grey earthenware with slip or pigments
ht: 8 to 20 cm

A common occurrence in Han tombs is the presence of domestic animals, no doubt echoing the appearance of the deceased's farmyards.

Domestic fowl is well represented here in fig. 46, 49 and 50, with a duck and ducklings, a goose, two roosters and a hen. A boar (fig. 48) and a watchdog (fig. 47) complete the lively picture.

Most of these small animals seem to have been mass-produced in twin moulds and the two separate, identical parts then luted together with the join quite visible. Sometimes, features were given added emphasis by modelling; the bristles on the back, ears, face and neck of the boar are a good example of this technique. The dog in fig. 47 is covered in white slip and most of the animals show some trace of red or white pigment.

49

47

48

Painted Pottery

51.

51. A Set of Entertainers
Eastern Han..........*Greyish-brown earthenware with red and black pigments*
ht: 8.5 to 10.8 cm

53. Seated Musicians
Eastern Han..........*Grey earthenware with red and white pigments*
ht: 13 to 18 cm

Musicians, dancers, singers, all were part of the larger tableau of entertainers who participated in Han funerals as well as feasts. Sometimes, figures of spectators would be included in the scene: seated at the periphery they could enjoy the antics of clowns and acrobats as well as the dance performances for which the orchestra provided the accompaniment.
Among these figures, musicians with wind or string instruments are clearly distinguishable. In fig.51, the two dancers are thought to be engaged in a dramatic rendition of the **qipan** *dance, where the performers must pivot on seven overturned bowls (now missing), agilely leaping from one bowl to another.*

53.

Painted Pottery

54. Dancer
Han..........Grey earthenware
ht: 26.2 cm

With a characteristic upturned face, the figurine falls into the curious category of one-armed dancers found in Han tombs. The left shoulder is invariably sliced off, but some specimens have been found with an opening for the insertion of a removable limb. Highly simplified, the angular form of these dancers in tubular robes emphasizes the strong linear movement of the torso; the line of the bent right arm and the flared skirt act to arrest and balance the dramatic swing of the body to the left.

55. Dancer
Han..........Grey earthenware with black and white pigments
ht: 26.5 cm

The form is similar to Fig. 54, but the head and torso are less angled.

Painted Pottery

57

57. Standing Figure
Western Han..........Grey earthenware with white pigment
ht: 22.4 cm

The elaborate form of the high headdress is the most striking feature of this figure, who stands with hands clasped together in front of his chest. Probably a dignitary, this smiling figure wears a long loose robe which is belted at the waist. Below the waist, the robe is incised with vertical lines to indicate separate sewn panels.
The figure is moulded and hollow.

56. Dancer (left)
Han..........Grey earthenware, burnished
ht: 24.8 cm

The conception is similar to that of fig.54 and fig.55. However, in silhouette, the torso shows a more sinuous movement, and is less severe in line. Facial features like the eyes and nose were probably added after moulding.
The figure has been constructed with the usual two-piece mould.

56. Dancer (right)
Han..........Grey earthenware
ht: 22.8 cm

With hair dressed like the one-armed dancers, this figure also wears a similar long robe which flares out towards the feet. Her pose is more natural and unforced, however: although her body is turned towards the left, she looks straight ahead, and swings out both arms in a wide arc, revealing the line of the capacious sleeves.
The figure has been made with a two-part mould.

56

Painted Pottery

59

59. Entertainers
Eastern Han..........Grey earthenware with red and black pigments
ht: 20 to 23 cm

*While these figures approach the grotesque, they are all expressive and dynamic. Their antics and sad or humorous stories must have entranced many a listener.
The standard mode of dress is a low-slung pair of trousers, sometimes tied by a red sash, with a large rounded belly protruding above. Bodies and heads were moulded in two halves, lengthwise.*

60. Entertainers
Eastern Han..........Grey earthenware with black and red pigments, slipped
ht: 17 and 16.3 cm

These two caricature-like entertainers convey movement in spite of their coarsely-moulded figures. Even the clown's whimsical expression has been captured.

60

63. **Entertainer**
Eastern Han..........Grey earthenware
ht: 18 cm

The male figure is roughly moulded, and stands with legs spread apart. The proportions are misshapen. Like similar figures, it is only clad in a pair of loose trousers, fastened below the pot-belly. Originally painted, the clay sculpture shows no trace of the unfired and perishable pigments. Seams along the sides of the body are indications that the figure was moulded in two sections.

63

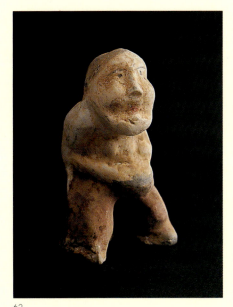
62

62. **Entertainer**
Eastern Han..........Grey earthenware with red, white and black pigments
ht: 16 cm

The roughly modelled figure has a misshapen head; it is depicted in an aggressive stance with legs apart. The jaw is outthrust as if trading insults.

61. **Entertainer**
Eastern Han..........Grey earthenware with black and red pigments, slipped
ht: 19.4 cm

The comic male figure is depicted in a rhythmic off-centre posture. He is attired only in a pair of loose trousers, flared at the bottom. He throws his head back with a pleading expression and rubs his pot belly.
The moulded figure is hollow.

61

Painted Pottery

58. **Balladeer with Drum** →
Eastern Han..........*Grey earthenware with red, black and white pigments*
ht: 40 cm

This figure with the lugubrious expression represents one of the practitioners of the performance called **shuochang** *which involves both talking and singing. He is clearly clowning: using hunched shoulders, a raised eyebrow, furrowed brow and a down-turned mouth to emphasize the sadness of the tale he accompanies on his circular drum. His costume consists of a peaked skull cap, a tunic, trousers which widen at the lower edge, and a bangle around his upper left arm. The skillful delineation of posture, gesture and facial expression of this balladeer typifies that seen in the evocative pottery sculptures of entertainers excavated in Sichuan Province.*

Painted Pottery

65

64, 65 & 66. **Warriors**
Late Eastern Han or later..........Grey or buff earthenware with white, red and black pigments
ht: 25 cm to 40.2 cm

All of these tomb guardians are pictured in a somewhat menacing position with right arm upraised, ready to throw a (missing) lance. In all but the shorter warrior in fig.64, the menacing gesture is further emphasized by an aggressive facial expression including a toothy grimace.

There is a stamped fish-scale pattern on the armoured tunic of the warrior on the left in fig.64. The warrior in fig.65 wears a short cross-over belted tunic and fitting trousers. His long hair is bound in three places into an impressive tall topknot.

The warrior in fig.66 has a bulbous nose and large bulging eyes. He wears a close-fitting, sectioned helmet with side and back flaps, topped by a mushroom-shaped finial. His belted corselet has a stamped fish-scale pattern and short sleeves edged with an incised band. Fig.66 is hollowed out from below, along the inner side of the legs.

66

64

Painted Pottery

67

67. **Dog**
Eastern Han..........Brownish-red earthenware with red, black and white pigments
ht: 25 cm, length: 22.5 cm

The animal's surface shows traces of red, white and black pigments used to delineate physical features as well as decorations.
Large red circles surrounding the eyeballs give the dog a friendly yet alert expression; the snub-nose, mouth and tongue are painted red, the muzzle, lips and whiskers black. Both red and black pigments are found inside the ears. A ribbon collar with trailing tassels in red and black seems to indicate a privileged position for this animal in the deceased's household.
It is made from a two-part mould.

Painted Pottery

68

68. Horse
Western Han..........*Grey earthenware with black and red pigments*
ht: 30 cm, length: 34 cm

This stout-looking animal has traces of black pigment on body and eyes, and red pigment on mouth and hooves.
In addition to the moulded saddle and saddle cloth, a bulbous appendage of indeterminate nature has been luted on to his nose.

69. Horse
Western Han..........*Grey earthenware*
ht: 31 cm, length: 32 cm

Another stout-looking animal similar in stance to fig.68, with straight forelegs and flexed hind legs. It is probably representative of the native Chinese breed of horses used widely before the famous Ferghana horses from Central Asia began to be imported into China.
In addition to the saddle and blanket, a shaped mane has been moulded as part of the decoration. There is also the indication of a bit. The horse is made from a bivalve mould and has an opening at the abdomen.

69

70

70. Horse
Western Han..........*Grey earthenware with a cream-coloured slip and red and white pigments*
ht: 39.5 cm, length: 39.5 cm

A cream-coloured slip covers the animal and white pigment outlines the harness and the saddle bags, the latter decorated in red. The mane has been coloured black.
The body has been moulded in two parts; the legs were added separately. This horse probably also represents the low steppe breed of Chinese horses.

Painted Pottery

71

71. **Tricorn**
Late Eastern Han or later..........Grey earthenware with white slip and red pigment
ht: 18.5 cm, length: 32 cm

Fig.71 is one of two tomb guardians with three "horns" protruding on the back of the head and neck.
The lowered head, curled-back tail and flexed rear legs give this small moulded animal an air of tenaciousness and steadfastness.
Eyes, mouth, jowls, ears and hooves form part of the moulded details. A spiral shape on the rump is representative of the animal's musculature.
The body is hollow with a large opening on the underside.

72

72. **Tricorn**
Late Eastern Han or later..........Grey earthenware with white slip and black and red pigments
ht: 28.7 cm, length: 36 cm

Moulded features such as ribs, eyes and hooves are given heightened prominence in black and red pigments.
This tricorn has been formed in a lengthwise bivalve mould which clearly delineates its anatomical features, particularly the ribs. In addition to these realistic features, there is a row of five button-shaped appliques along the spine, plus one on each shoulder and two on the rump.

73. **Bull**
Late Eastern Han or later..........Grey earthenware with white slip and traces of red pigment
ht: 23.4 cm, length: 32 cm

The bull's head is lowered, almost to the ground, as if ready to charge. A noteworthy feature of this bull is the crescent-shaped appendage on its back, flanked by two curved, horn-like supports. The horn-like motif is repeated once on the right side of the body and twice on the left; it is also repeated twice on the back of the neck. A narrow slit appears along the concave section of the crescent.
The hollow body has a large opening on the abdomen.

73

Painted Pottery

74.

74. Stove
Eastern Han..........Light-grey earthenware with brown ash glaze
ht: 18 cm, length: 23 cm

An arched opening at the vertical front panel of the rectangular stove is designed for feeding fuel to the fire chamber; beside this opening kneels a roughly sculpted figure. The upper surface of the stove has two apertures into which pots can be set. A dog at the far end guards the cooking range, near which is a vertical protruberance resembling the head and long neck of an animal. This protruberance probably served as the flue or chimney. The two long vertical sides of the stove are ornamented by incised intersecting lines, and an undecipherable incised mark is also seen on the side below the dog.

75.

75. Jar
Eastern Han..........Grey earthenware with brown ash glaze
ht: 20 cm, dia: 20 cm

Traces of ash glaze adhere to impressions made by fabric on the upper body to a point below the mid-line. There are irregularly-spaced stamped circles enclosing chevron patterns and some drips of greenish glaze, perhaps unintentional. The lid has a simple knob handle, and the body has four horizontal loop handles. The base of the jar is flat.

76. Lidded Bowl ➔
Eastern Han.........Ash-glazed earthenware
ht: 19.2 cm, dia: 24.5 cm

The dark brown glaze has olive green areas on one side, congealing thickly on the foot.
The lid has a flattened top with a lug and loose ring attachment, and stamped and incised arcuate motifs enclosed within thin incised circles. Dumbbell-shaped slots have been cut into the vessel's vertical collar. The body too has incised circles and other motifs.
The foot has a circle of thin glaze in the centre, and traces of six kiln supports.

Painted Pottery

77. Hu
Eastern Han..........*Pale-buff earthenware with brown ash glaze*
ht: 26.5 cm, dia: 20 cm

The brownish glaze contains flecks of darker colour and a greenish crackled splash on one side of the neck. The glazed lid was chiselled after firing to remove it from the neck to which it had become stuck.
The stepped lid has a ring attachment holding a ring handle. There are two lug handles on the shoulder. Two double incised lines appear on the shoulder and at the midpoint.
The hollow flaring foot has two perforations at the junction with the body. There are remains of thin glaze in a circle on the underside of the base.

80. Jarlet
Eastern Han..........*Ash-glazed earthenware*
ht: 10.5 cm, dia: 13.7 cm, dia (mouth): 3 cm

A simple jar, the only decoration being two lug handles.

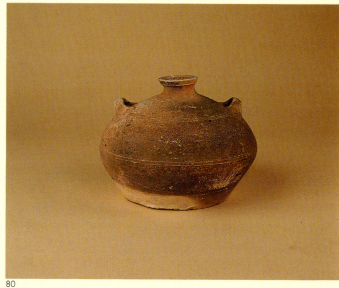

78. Lidded Jar
Eastern Han..........*Buff earthenware with brown ash glaze*
ht: 16 cm, dia: 16.7 cm

The mottled brownish glaze covers the jar unevenly on one side, while on the other it dwindles to expose the biscuit. The upper body beneath the lid is unglazed. The glaze of the lid is relatively more evenly applied. This phenomenon suggests that glazing was directional, due to ash caught in an updraft in the kiln.
Lumps appear on the body, probably due to impurities in the clay.

The simple decoration consists of double parallel lines around the upper body and at the midpoint, and four lug handles.
The flat base bears traces of four kiln supports and has a thin glaze.

Painted Pottery

79

79. Cup with Lid

Eastern Han..........Ash-glazed pinkish-buff earthenware
ht: 11.2 cm, dia (cup) 10.1 cm, dia (lid): 10.4 cm

A brownish glaze covers the lid and part of the cup. The sides of the cup bulge slightly below the double-loop handle. The cup is supported on three stubby feet. The three-stepped lid is surmounted by a ring attachment and a loose ring handle, undoubtedly based on those found on metal vessels. Similar cups have been found in lacquer with metal fittings.
On the unglazed base are double incised rings, possibly for positioning the three feet.

Painted Pottery

Glazed Pottery

81. **Dog**
Eastern Han..........Red earthenware with an amber glaze
ht: 25 cm, length: 25 cm

The exaggerated neck and raised head give this dog an air of alertness. Its mouth is open, its ears bent forward. Whiskers and skin folds on jowls are incised. Except for the head, the animal displays few detailed physical characterics, however there is a tiny moulded paw which protrudes from the middle of the body and a hint of a tail.

82. **Dog**
Eastern Han...........Orange earthenware with an amber glaze
ht: 20.3 cm, length: 35 cm

Here is a burly animal, with a broad neck, prominent haunches, and heavy legs and paws.
Incised features include fur around its face and ears, whiskers, eyelashes, brow, nose, jowls and paws. An incised line also runs down the middle of the face. The nostrils and ears are pierced and the bushy tail fans out.

83. **Hu**
Eastern Han..........Amber-glazed red earthenware
ht: 37 cm, dia: 27.5 cm, dia (mouth): 15.5 cm

84. **Hu**
Late Eastern Han..........Olive green-glazed red earthenware
ht: 31 cm, dia (mouth): 12.5 cm

Each "hu" depicts within its shoulder frieze a hunting scene with various wild or mythical animals chasing each other in an endless circle. On fig. 83, wavy lines represent a mountainous landscape. Two "taotie" masks are incorporated into the moulded frieze of each "hu".

83

85. **Hu**
Late Eastern Han..........Amber-glazed red earthenware
ht: 24 cm, dia: 20 cm, dia (mouth): 20 cm

The globular jar rises to a dished mouth. There are two grooves below the lip and two incised bands on the rounded shoulder. Three spur marks are visible on the rim. The concave base is glazed but the interior of the jar is unglazed.

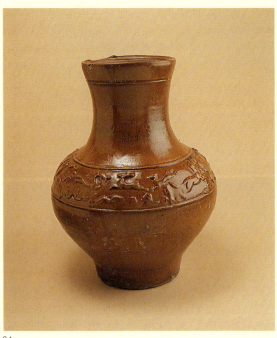

84

85

Glazed Pottery

86

87

86 & 87. Granaries
Late Eastern Han..........Amber-glazed red earthenware
86. ht: 24 cm, dia (roof): 18 cm
87. ht: 32 cm, dia: 16 cm

Fig. 86 and 87 are similar in many respects. Bands of triple grooves encircle the tapering bodies. The flaring, slightly domed roofs are moulded to represent a series of radiating tile covers with three rows of flat tiles in between. Both vessels are supported by moulded bear feet. The granary in fig. 86 has a crackled glaze with areas of silvery iridescence.

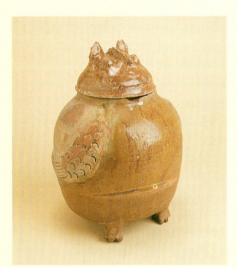
88

88. Owl-shaped Covered Jar
Late Eastern Han..........Red earthenware with a greenish-brown glaze
ht: 20 cm, dia: 12 cm

The oviform jar represents the owl's body. The wings are moulded in such a way that the wingtips protrude beyond the vessel wall. The domed lid represents the bird's head, with modelled upright "ears", bulging eyes and hooked beak. The base is flat, supported by the bird's three-clawed feet and a short tail.

89. Hill Jar
Late Eastern Han..........Green-glazed red earthenware
ht: 28 cm, dia: 21.5 cm

90. Hill Jar
Eastern Han..........Red earthenware with amber glaze
ht: 26 cm, dia: 22 cm

The lids in fig. 89 and 90 illustrate a mountain theme where fauna disport themselves. The lid in fig. 89 has a "pie-crust" edge.
In fig. 89 the central band on the jar is incised with birds and other animals, and dancers. Three birds with outspread wings form the feet. The moulded frieze on the body of fig. 90 depicts a hunting scene and includes two **taotie** masks. Three bear feet support the jar.

89

90

Glazed Pottery

91.

91. **Hill Jar**
Eastern Han.........Red earthenware with a bluish-green glaze
ht: 24 cm, dia: 19.5 cm

The underside of the lid is unglazed except for four splashes at the apex. The moulded lid rises to five peaks amidst which cavort a horse, striped tiger, two rams, a dragon and a man holding a branch-like object. There are spur marks on the upper surface of the lid. The moulded frieze on the body is composed of two similar sections, each depicting a large fierce feline, and small figures of rams and a man holding a branch-like object. There are spur marks on the rim of the body.
The base is unglazed. Three bear feet support the jar.

Glazed Pottery

92.

92. Tripod Jar
Late Eastern Han..........*Orange-red earthenware with amber and green glazes*
ht: 19 cm, dia: 21.7 cm, dia (mouth) : 7.2 cm

The glaze is flaking and degraded in parts and the body is slightly powdery in texture.
The body is decorated with several sets of incised lines: two sets of two and one on the amber body, two wide grooves and one incised line on the green shoulder, and another groove on the upper shoulder. The jar is supported by three unglazed zoomorphic feet with earth adhesions.

93. Pair of Hu
Late Eastern Han..........*Orange earthenware with amber and green glazes*
ht: both 18.5 cm, dia: 15 cm and 14 cm, dia (mouth): 5.6 and 5 cm respectively

The very thin glaze varies from uneven green to amber.
Decoration is confined to incised lines on the shoulders.

93.

Glazed Pottery

95. **Hu**
Eastern Han..........*Reddish earthenware with a green glaze*
ht: 37.5 cm, dia: 26.5 cm, dia (mouth): 12.5 cm

The green glaze has several brown streaks in it, extending downward from the rim. The object has been repainted in several places.
The body has been moulded in two parts; the seam is visible below the decorative frieze.
Besides a groove around the mouthrim, the object is decorated with a moulded frieze enclosed within carved rings. The frieze contains two **taotie** *masks, a mounted bowman pursued by a beast, felines, bear-like figures, a dragon, wild boar and other animals in a mountainous landscape.*

95

94

94. **Cylindrical Pot**
Late Eastern Han.........*Pink earthenware with a watery green glaze*
ht: 10.5 cm, dia: 15 cm

The pot is glazed inside and out, but otherwise undecorated.
The piling of the glaze and clay adhesions on the base suggest that the object was fired at an angle of sixty degrees.

Glazed Pottery

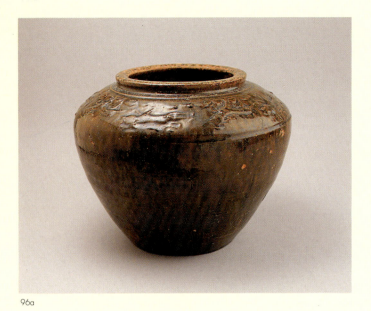
96a

96b

96. Guan
Eastern Han..........Reddish earthenware with a streaked green glaze
ht: 16 cm, dia: 21 cm

The transparent glaze with green streaks reveals the reddish body beneath. The base is also glazed.
The decoration consists of a relief carving between the mouth and shoulder featuring animals in procession, possibly a deer pursued by a stag. The orientation of the animals is unusual in that their heads point outwards, their feet towards the jar mouth.

98

98. Lian
Eastern Han..........Pinkish-buff earthenware with a yellowish glaze
ht: 17.5 cm, dia: 18.5 cm

The lid has a silvery iridescence with opalescent blue highlights, while the glaze of the body is yellowish with dark-green streaks and one area of brownish colour.
*The lid is moulded with a four-petalled flower in the center. The body is adorned with two moulded **taotie** masks with mouth rings, and two sets of incised lines at the rim and mid-section.*
The object has three well-moulded bear feet with beards and pointed ears. The base is cord-cut and thinly glazed, with iridescence near the edge.

Glazed Pottery

97

97.Cylindrical Tripod
Mid Eastern Han..........Buff earthenware with a reddish-green glaze
ht: 14.2 cm, dia: 20.5 cm

The tripod is coated with an unusual lead glaze varying from wine to reddish-green to brown, with gold iridescence in one corner.
Decoration is confined to two horizontal grooves just beneath the rim, and three broad grooves on the interior.
The base is unglazed. The feet are stylized bears, reduced to one sphere stacked on top of another. The undersides of the feet have standard wedge-shaped spur remnants.

Glazed Pottery

99.

99. **Hu**
Western Han..........Red earthenware with a streaky green glaze
ht: 39 cm, dia: 37 cm, dia (mouth): 20.5 cm

The overall green colour of the glaze reveals the faint traces of the underlying red body in streaks.
*Two moulded **taotie** masks are affixed with rings and an unusual beaded decoration. There are sets of grooves at the mid-line, the junction of body and neck, and one at the base.*

100. **Guan**
Eastern Han..........Reddish earthenware with a streaky green glaze
ht: 16 cm, dia: 18 cm

The undecorated jar is angled at the shoulder, slanting up to a low mouthrim.
The glazed base shows three spur marks.

100.

Glazed Pottery

101

101. **Dish**
Late Eastern Han..........*Red earthenware, glazed green with* **sancai** *effect*
ht: 2.3 cm, dia: 10.7 cm

The dish is plain and unornamented. On the flat rim are three spur marks. A slightly raised foot surrounds the flat base.

102. **Sheep Pen**
Eastern Han..........*Amber and green-glazed earthenware*
ht: 6 cm, dia: 20.5 cm

Three rams with clearly moulded hind and fore quarters are sitting up in a basin-like pen. The basin, which has a carinated profile, is pierced with seven small holes.
There are some areas of silvery-white iridescence in the interior of the pen and the underside edge of the cord-cut base. The body is reddish in colour, except for the firing scar on the floor of the pen which has turned a darker red.

104

102

104. **Farmer with Hoe**
Late Eastern Han..........*Amber-glazed buff earthenware with green streaks*
ht: 27 cm

Holding a two-pronged hoe in his hands, this Han farmer is depicted with a top-knot and prominent nose; he appears to have a cropped beard. The topknot is a style also found on acrobats and athletes. He wears a wrap-over tunic reaching to just below the knees. Shoes are discernible under his narrow trousers.
The body is moulded in two longitudinal sections.

Glazed Pottery

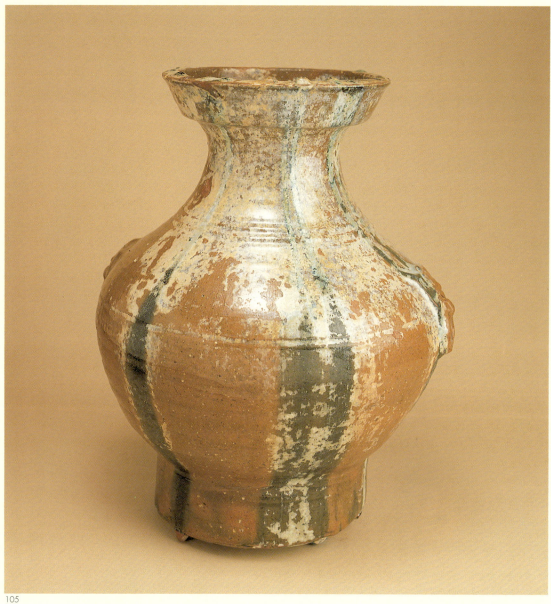

105. **Hu**
Late Eastern Han..........*Brown and green-glazed red earthenware with iridescence*
ht: 35.5 cm, dia: 25 cm

The exterior is covered in a brown glaze with vertical streaks of green; the interior is brown only.
The decoration consists of two moulded **taotie** *masks on the midsection, set over a groove. There are also three slightly raised lines on the base of the neck. The base is supported on three knife-edged spur-like feet.*

Glazed Pottery

103

103. **Horse**
Late Eastern Han.........Red earthenware with amber and green glazes
ht: 13.2 cm, length:14 cm

The extremely well-preserved glaze of this small, almost toy-like horse or pony is amber on the head and feet and green on the other parts of the body.
All features of the animal, its mane, harness and saddle are moulded. Decoration on the saddle itself may be incised.

Glazed Pottery

106. **Hu**
Late Eastern Han..........*Brown-glazed red earthenware*
ht: 20 cm, dia: 14 cm

The unusual decoration consists of green-glazed lines over-painted on the brown glaze around the mouthrim, shoulder and mid-section, and zigzag lines on the neck. There are also irregular blotches of green at the shoulder. Moulded bands of parallel lines can be detected under the green-glazed decoration on the shoulder and mid-section.

107 & 108. **Hu**
Eastern Han..........*Green-glazed red earthenware*
107. ht: 37 cm
108. ht: 37 cm, dia: 28 cm, dia (mouth): 15 cm

Hunting scenes with men on horseback and prancing animals are depicted on these two **hu**. *Two* **taotie** *masks complement the moulded frieze in each case.*
Both **hu** *were formed by moulding two parts which are joined horizontally at the mid-sections of the vessels. Spur marks are to be found on the base of each* **hu** *as well as on the rim of fig. 108. Fig. 108 shows some traces of iridescence.*

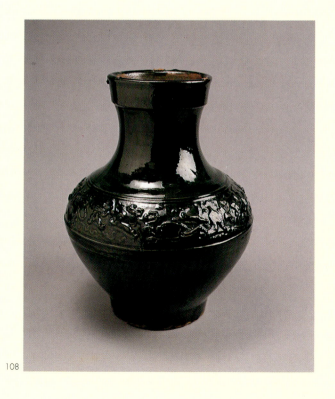

Glazed Pottery

109. **Ding Tripod**
Late Western Han...........*Pinkish-buff earthenware with a green glaze*
ht: 17.4 cm, dia: 20 cm, dia (with projections): 23.4 cm

The glaze varies from yellowish to dark green. The interior of the lid is thinly glazed and possesses gritty adhesions and three spur marks. The exterior of the body is fully glazed, except for the bases of the feet. The interior is partially coated with a thin glaze. There are three spur marks on the rim of the vessel.
Decoration is confined to simple modelling, including a knob on the top of the lid, and three tooth-like projections halfway between the knob and the rim. The body is decorated with a low medial horizontal flange.

109

110. **Ding Tripod**
Early to Mid Western Han..........*Green-glazed red earthenware*
ht (with lid): 18.7 cm, dia (with handles): 21.5 cm,
dia (mouth): 12.7 cm

The highly iridescent glaze is green on the exterior, amber on the interior. Glaze is irregularly splashed on the interior of the lid.
The cover has a complex moulded decoration consisting of a central motif of two crossed fish. In the sharper angles thus formed are crab-like creatures, in the wider angles are set human or bird-like shapes. The lower portion of the lid forms a horizontal band of scrollwork vaguely resembling a cloud scroll but of a regular stylized design among which irregularly spaced beads are dispersed. The typical three spur marks appear on the cloud scroll band.
The lower body is undecorated but for a raised ridge at the widest point. The object rests on three simple feet with well-preserved wedges on the bottoms, which are glazed.

110

Glazed Pottery

111

112

111, 112 & 113. **Ding Tripods**
Mid Western Han...........Green-glazed red earthenware
ht: 15 to 20 cm

*The tripods in fig. 111 and 113 are almost identical in their decoration to the tripod in fig. 110. However, incised triangles have been added just below the rim of fig. 113. Both vessels show some iridescence.
A moulded frieze on the lid of fig. 112 represents the familiar Daoist abode of the Immortals: a mountainous landscape with hunter and wild animals and birds. The frieze encircles a pair of dragons and the knob at the centre has a moulded ring recalling bronze prototypes. Solid S-shaped handles are attached to the body which rests on moulded bear feet.*

113

115. **Granary Jar** ➤
Eastern Han..........Green-glazed red earthenware with iridescence
ht: 34.5 cm, dia: 24 cm, dia (opening): 9 cm

*In overall design, this granary is similar to fig. 114. The decoration is however enriched by lightly stamped motifs which are faintly visible under the glaze.
The glaze has acquired a full, silvery iridescence.*

Glazed Pottery

114

114. Granary Jar
Eastern Han..........*Light-pink earthenware with dark-green glaze*
ht: 33.5 cm, dia (roof): 24 cm, outer dia (mouth): 6.8 cm

This vessel seems to be a partial representation of actual granaries constructed during Han times.
The mouth at the top of the vessel, the lid that accompanies some pieces, and the moulded bear feet suggest that this basic form had been adapted to more practical use as a ritual container.
Three sets of grooves are carved around the sides. The flaring roof has four short hip ridges.
The base of the jar and the lower parts of the three bear feet are unglazed.

117. Hill Censer →
Early to Mid Eastern Han...........*Red earthenware with an iridescent green glaze*
ht: 23 cm, dia (saucer): 21 cm

The separable top depicts a forest scene where felines, deer, birds, and other animals roam, with a lower border of repeated three concentric triangles. The base is a plain bowl, hollow stem, and saucer.
The foot is formed of three plain flanges.

116. Grain Jar
Eastern Han..........*Red earthenware with an iridescent green glaze*
ht: 32.5 cm, dia: 16 cm, dia (mouth): 10.5 cm

The shape of this jar is very similar to that of the granary jars (fig. 86, 87, 114, 115) except that it lacks a flared roof and bear feet, and has more steeply sloping shoulders, and sides which taper down to a slightly recessed, solid foot. It is not clear whether this vessel is intended to be a model of a granary. However, as grain has been found inside similar excavated vessels, this is almost certainly a grain jar.
The interior and base are unglazed.

116

Glazed Pottery

118

120

118. Tripod
Eastern Han..........Red earthenware with an iridescent green glaze
ht (with cover): 19.3 cm, ht (without cover): 14.6 cm, dia: 19.2 cm, dia (mouth): 9 cm

The flat top of the lid is decorated with a motif of three criss-cross lines, and perforated by five circles. The sides of the lid have two **taotie** masks with rings and an aquatic scene including three egrets, four fish, and swirling lines suggesting water plants. The body is plain except for a thick flange around the midpoint. There are three spur marks on the body's lip. The object rests on three tubular feet.

120. Dish
Eastern Han..........Red earthenware with a highly iridescent dark-green glaze
dia: 13.7 cm

The moulded dish has a square-cut rim on which three spur marks are visible. A groove circles the interior of the cavetto. There is a moulded design of scrolled waves on the exterior wall, framed by two serrated bands.
The glazed base of the dish is slightly concave, with three spur marks and a ring in the centre.

122. Hill Jar
Eastern Han..........Red earthenware with a light apple-green glaze
ht (with lid): 26.5 cm, dia: 20.5 cm

The glaze covers the interior and exterior of both lid and body. The glaze on the interior of the lid is limited to four streaks of glaze radiating from the highest point.
The lid depicts a central peak surrounded by four subsidiary peaks with dragons, phoenixes, and other mythical beasts in relief in between the peaks.
The body consists of a moulded frieze depicting

122

four felines with figures hovering above their backs, monkeys, boars, **kilin** style animals and other beasts amid a mountainous landscape, as well as two **taotie** masks holding rings.
The bottom is unglazed, and displays two adhesions which are probably spur marks. The feet depict bears.

Glazed Pottery

119

119. *Tripod*
Eastern Han..........*Buff earthenware with a highly iridescent green glaze*
ht (without lid): 15 cm, ht (with lid): 19 cm,
dia: 19.5 cm, dia (mouth): 8.5 cm, dia (lid): 10.3 cm

The tripod is completely glazed on the exterior. The interior has only splashes of glaze. The exterior glaze of the lid is thin and without iridescence.
The upper body is richly decorated with a moulded frieze including two riders on galloping horses, hill motifs, a dragon, and a fierce feline. The lower border of the frieze is marked by a flange, the upper by a row of triangles.
The lid consists of four groups of three peaks surrounding a central group of five peaks.
The object rests on three simple feet.

Glazed Pottery

123

123. Hill Jar
Eastern Han..........*Red earthenware with a highly iridescent green glaze*
ht (with lid): 23.4 cm, ht (without lid): 15.6 cm, dia: 19.5 cm

The exterior of the jar is glazed green; the base interior more amber in tone.
*The lid bears a motif of seventeen peaks among which frolic riders on horseback, and various other beings. The outer surfaces of the mountains depict trees in silhouette. At the rim is a border of triangles and three wedge-shaped spur marks, with three more spur marks on the underside of the lid. The body bears a decorative frieze stamped in two sections, containing a multitude of creatures: a dragon, a bear, birds, charging boars, tigers and other unidentifiable quadrupeds. In the frieze are two **taotie** masks with rings. There are three spur marks on the top of the body's rim, and three more on the upper surface of the lid's rim. The object stands on three bear-shaped feet.*

121. Lian ➝
Middle Han..........*Red earthenware with a highly iridescent green glaze*
ht: 17.5 cm, dia: 20 cm

*The lid is decorated with moulded motifs including a four-petalled flower in the centre, surrounded by seventeen triangles and a wavy scroll design. At the lower edge of the lid are more triangles. There are three spur marks on the upper surface of the lid. The decoration of the body is confined to double incised lines at the upper lip and midpoint, and two **taotie** masks with attached ring. The object is supported by three roughly-moulded bear feet.*

Glazed Pottery

124

124 & 125. **Bowls with Handle**
Eastern Han..........*Red earthenware with an iridescent green glaze*
124. ht: 10.7 cm
125. ht: 9 cm

Although the handles suggest their use as ladles, these two similar Han vessels were ewers for water. Decoration is minimal: the rims have been pinched in, giving them a somewhat squarish appearance and on fig. 124, two incised bands circle the exterior of the bowl, below the rim. The marked pooling of glaze inside both bowls suggests that they were fired at an angle. Spur marks are visible on both.

125

126

126 & 127. **Ladles**
Eastern Han..........*Green-glazed red earthenware*
length: 11 to 13.3 cm

The handle of the ladle on the right in fig. 126 is in the shape of a round-eyed long-necked monster with wrinkled snout curving up at the end; the animal's teeth are biting a ball modelled in its mouth. The gracefully curved handle of the ladle on the left in fig. 126 is sculpted.
The ladle on the left of fig. 127 has a high and sharply angled handle. The spoon and handle on the right recall the form of a gourd sliced down the middle.

127

Glazed Pottery

129a

129. **Earcup**

Eastern Han..........*Reddish earthenware with an iridescent green glaze*
ht: 4.5 cm, width: 9.5 cm, length: 10 cm

The vessel is completely glazed. The interior of the earcup is undecorated. The main design on the exterior wall of the earcup shows scrolling waves. Above this, running below the rim of the vessel, is a border pattern comprising repeated circles within squares. A phoenix in flight, with outstretched wings, forms an unexpected and beguiling ornamentation on the oval base.

129b

Glazed Pottery

128

130

128 & 130. **Earcups**
Eastern Han..........Green-glazed earthenware
length: 11 to 13.7 cm

The pottery earcup is based on lacquer models of wine vessels. The two wing-like appendages which flank the vessel are designed for grasping in the hands.
The piling of glaze on one side of the interior in fig. 128 suggests that the vessel was probably fired at an angle of forty-five degrees. On the other hand, the two earcups in fig. 130 show spur marks on the "ears", suggesting that two vessels were fired together, rim to rim.

131

131 & 132. **Dishes**
Eastern Han..........Pinkish earthenware with a green, highly iridescent glaze
dia: 17 cm

The dish in fig. 131 has a rounded rim but is otherwise unornamented. An interesting feature of the flat unglazed base is the presence of a small hole, 1.5 cm in diameter, which is surrounded by a raised ridge.
The dish interior in fig. 132 is marked by a shallow circular depression in the centre.
The outstanding feature of these two plain vessels is their high degree of iridescence.

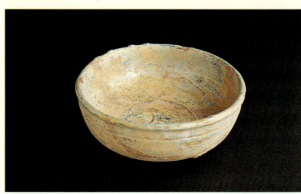
132

Glazed Pottery

133.

133. **Brazier and Pot**
Eastern Han..........Red earthenware with an iridescent leaf-green glaze
(Stove) ht: 13 cm, dia: 17 cm
(Pot) ht: 11 cm, dia: 14 cm

Three prongs on the rim of the circular brazier are positioned to support a cooking or heating utensil. A triangular aperture at the front of the cylindrical lower section is used for fueling the fire-chamber. The globular cooking pot which sits on the brazier has a slanting handle with a hooked end; the moulding of its cover suggests the configuration of mountain peaks found on the covers of "hill jars." The construction of this Han brazier looks familiar because its form is echoed in portable Chinese charcoal stoves still in use in the twentieth century.

134.

135.

134. **Brazier**
Eastern Han..........Red earthenware with a dark-green, partly iridescent glaze
ht: 12 cm, dia (top): 21 cm, dia (base): 11.5 cm

The upper part of the brazier is globular, ending in a circular slab with fourteen holes. Below the slab is the smaller fuel compartment. A small semi-circular opening on one side serves for feeding and stoking the fire. There are three spur marks on the flat rim of the brazier.
Around the edge of the glazed base are congealed droplets of glaze; the fact that three spur marks are found both on the top as well as on the base suggests that the braziers were fired in a stack, top to top and base to base.

135. **Brazier**
Eastern Han..........Red earthenware with a glossy dark-green glaze
ht: 12 cm, dia: 17.7 cm

The circular brazier has eight rectangular slits in the horizontal slab set into the interior, and three openings on the cavetto. There are two grooves around the exterior of the foot and two at the lip.
The unglazed base shows a high circular foot. A triangular opening cut into the base serves as an air-vent.

Glazed Pottery

136a

136. Brazier with Roasting Cicadas
Eastern Han..........Orange-red earthenware with a green glaze, showing some iridescence
ht:10.5 cm, length: 23.5 cm, width: 15.5 cm

*Standing on four bear feet, this rectangular brazier has an overhanging flat rim. Extensive moulded decoration can be seen along its sides. These include diagonal criss-cross panels incorporating bosses, four **taotie** masks with rings, a hunting scene with men and an assortment of animals. On each of two bars stretching across the brazier rim are four roasting cicadas. Two smaller cicadas can also be found on the base of the brazier. Although jade cicadas were used in Han funerary rites as symbols of rejuvenation, the cicadas modelled in this pottery brazier may not possess a symbolic meaning. Most likely, they simply represent a regional delicacy relished for its taste and texture, for crisply roasted cicadas are reportedly still served today as an appetizer in northeastern China. On the unglazed feet of the brazier are wedge-shaped spurs.*

136b

Glazed Pottery

137. **Brazier**
Eastern Han..........Pinkish-red earthenware with a green glaze
ht: 9 cm, dia: 15.5 cm

The brazier has a bowl-shaped top section. The circular slab forming the base of the bowl is pierced with nineteen round holes. The narrower lower section of the brazier has a semi-circular opening through which charcoal can be placed. The flat unglazed base shows traces of cord-marking and three spur marks.

137

138. **Steamer**
Eastern Han..........Reddish-brown earthenware with a streaky green glaze and brown spots, possibly iron inclusions
ht: 14.9 cm, dia (top): 23.6 cm, dia (base): 12.1 cm,
dia (holes): 1.8 cm

The vessel flares out sharply to a flat rim at the top. There are five holes in the base, which may have been stamped out. The perforations are most likely for steam or water to pass through, suggesting the use of the vessel as a Chinese **zeng** *or steamer. Such flower-pot-shaped steamers are seen in illustrations of Han cooking ranges, fitted into the top of rounded boilers. Sets of these two-tiered vessels were also made in metal. Marks circling the vessel indicate that it was thrown on the wheel. There are three spur marks on the glazed base.*

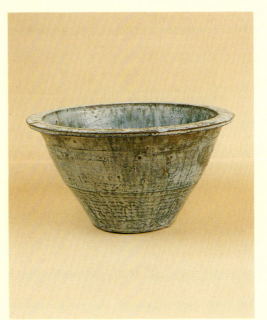 
138a 138b

Glazed Pottery

139.

139. Stove

Eastern Han.........Red earthenware with a thin green glaze
(Oven) ht: 8.5 cm
(Shed) ht: 19.6 cm

This unusual model incorporates a roofed shed which extends upwards from the back of the stove. Windows are cut into the shed at both front and back. Its tile roof is ridged and features eighteen round tile ends with a stamped wheel design. A small central protrusion on the rear roof projection may represent the flue for the stove.
The top of the stove has the usual circular opening to hold a cooking pot. An arched aperture in the vertical front panel leads into the fire-chamber. Stamped on the side walls and top surface of the stove are twenty-four repeat patterns with a stylized motif of three mountain peaks.
The stove model is open at the base and unglazed.

140. Stove

Eastern Han..........Pinkish earthenware with a thick green iridescent glaze
(Stove) ht: 10.6 cm, length: 27.5 cm, width: 19 cm
(Chimney) ht: 8 cm

The upper surface has three conical openings which extend into the interior of the stove and terminate in rounded bases. A chimney rises from the end, its interior continuous with the interior of the stove. A glazed jar is attached to the top of the stove, to the right of the chimney. The unusually thick glaze obscures what may be moulded objects on the stove surface.
The vertical front panel of the stove has a roughly cut rectangular opening for stoking. On either side, a moulded figure leans toward the opening. One of the figures holds a stick. Double raised lines frame the opening, above which is a geometric design.
The base of the stove shows some splashes of glaze. There are heavy earth adhesions on the unglazed underside.

140.

Glazed Pottery

141. **Stove**
Eastern Han..........*Reddish earthenware with a dark-green glaze*
ht: 19.5 cm, length: 27 cm

Three cooking pots are set into the top of the U-shaped range, with the shoulders and mouths protruding above the surface. A pot-shaped hollow chimney rises at one end. Next to it is a jar which is attached to the stove top. The vertical panel at the front of the stove has an entrance door to the hollowed out fire-chamber; above the door is a panel with a diagonally arranged ribbed pattern. Facing the entrance on either side is a kneeling figure wearing a pointed hat, moulded in high relief. One holds a stick-like object, the other a vessel or utensil.

At the base of the underside a band of buff-coloured slip can be seen.

142. **Stove**
Eastern Han..........*Reddish earthenware with an olive-green glaze*
ht: 10.5 cm, length: 18.2 cm, width: 17.8 cm

The stove is U-shaped, with a flat top ending in a ledge overhanging the opening to the fire-chamber. Two cooking pots are set into the stove top. Around the pots are a varied assortment of food and utensils, moulded in crisp relief: a hook and ladle placed face down, ring attachments for hanging, a lid, a whisk-like object, two large prawns, a pair of fish, a squash, a plate with three dumplings, another dish with a turtle, a third dish probably holding a fowl. The overhanging ledge is decorated with a frieze of X-shaped ribs in four panels, with a central panel incorporating bosses. Moulded in relief below the ledge are two kneeling figures who flank the door to the firebox. The left figure holds a stick, perhaps for stoking the fire.

Glazed Pottery

144. **Oil Lamp** →
Eastern Han..........*Green-glazed red earthenware*
ht: 50 cm, dia (base of dish): 33 cm

The central motif of this visually striking lamp is a long-necked bird with a small head. Feathers are depicted on the wings and tail. A hole under the tail may possibly be for a missing attachment. A hollow cylinder rises from the bird's back. The bird is supported on another cylinder which is joined below to a bowl with a flanged rim and a high flaring foot. The foot of the bowl is decorated in front with two carved motifs comprising intersecting lines.
On the square-lipped rim of the bowl, perforations receive the tails of four animals bearing cup-shaped saucers on their backs. Two of the animals have upward-curving front legs, suggesting flight; the other two have forelegs which curve downward toward the chest. Two perforations in the cavetto of the bowl probably held objects which are now missing.

143. **Stove**
Eastern Han..........*Red earthenware with an iridescent green glaze*
ht: 13 cm, width: 21.5 cm, length: 30.5 cm

Rectangular in section, the stove is framed by a decorative border, comprising twelve panels with X-shaped ribs incorporating bosses moulded in relief. Around the projecting shoulders of the three cooking pots moulded on the stove are a number of kitchen utensils, namely, a brush, a spoon, a scraper, a ladle, a hook and skewers. Among the items depicted appear to be a rectangular stand seen from the side, and a circular grill. At the front of the stove is a rectangular projection, centrally placed above the semi-circular opening to the fire-chamber. A ram's head with long curling horns adorns the space just behind the vertical projection. There is also a small vertical projection at the back of the stove surface, and a small horizontal ledge below and to the right of the firebox opening.
The base is open, showing an unglazed interior and foot.

Glazed Pottery

145. Incense Burner and Oil Lamp
Eastern Han..........Reddish earthenware with an iridescent green glaze
ht: 36 cm, dia (basin): 27 cm

This article consists of nine separate pieces: in the centre of the circular basin is a central stand for the incense burner, over which is placed the stem of the burner, a bowl to hold incense, and the lid of the burner. There are also four shallow saucers for holding oil, with curved stems which fit into apertures spaced along the flat rim of the basin.
The incense burner is of the **boshan lu** type: the domed lid is moulded in the form of mountain peaks, representing the abode of Daoist Immortals. Perforations in the lid allow the release of smoke from aromatic herbs or incense placed in the burner.
The base of the basin and the bases of the bowls for holding oil and incense are unglazed.

145

146

146. Oil Lamp
Eastern Han..........Red earthenware with a dark-green iridescent glaze
ht: 14.5 cm, dia: 11 cm

This portable oil lamp has a cylindrical stem for easy grasping. Purely functional in design, it is undecorated except for two wide grooves which circle the flaring base. Strikingly similar green-glazed lamps were used in Chinese homes in Singapore up to the beginning of the present century.
Two spur marks are visible on the rim of the saucer-shaped holder for oil.

Glazed Pottery

147

147. **Oil Lamp**
Eastern Han..........*Pinkish-buff earthenware with a green, iridescent glaze*
ht: 18 cm, dia (bowls): 8.7 cm

The hand-thrown lamp consists of three clustered bowls for holding oil. The bowls are joined together below a tall loop handle.
The cord-cut bases of the bowls are flat, and exhibit some glaze drippings. A small protrusion at the base of the centre portion shows where the loop of the handle was attached.
The mottled green glaze covering the lamp shows silvery and golden iridescence.

150. **Perfumer**
Eastern Han..........*Pinkish-buff earthenware with an apple-green glaze*
ht: 13.1 cm, dia:13.1 cm, dia (mouth): 4.2 cm

The perfumer has three horizontal rows of roughly cut perforations to diffuse the fragrance of herbs or spices placed in the vessel: upper and lower row perforations are triangular while the middle row has lozenge-shaped perforations.
On the rim of the perfumer are three spur marks and a wedge-shaped spur.
The slightly concave base is unglazed, but shows some overflow of glaze from the side of the container.

150

148

148. **Incense Burner**
Eastern Han.........*Pinkish-red earthenware with an iridescent mottled green glaze*
ht: 27.5 cm, dia: 13.2 cm

The body has three joints indicating that the object was made in four sections.
The non-detachable lid has four triangular projecting flaps which are incised to resemble leaf-like veins. The bud-shaped finial has four similar flaps and sits on a square slab.
The flat, unglazed base displays cord-cut marks.

Glazed Pottery

149

149. **Brazier**
Early Eastern Han..........*Pinkish-red earthenware with a degraded green glaze*
ht: 13.5 cm, length: 29 cm, width: 18.5 cm

This brazier consists of a rectangular section joined to a semi-circular section. It stands on a trio of squat animal feet, two placed below the junction of the two sections, and one below the centre of the rectangular end. A band of incised diamonds decorates the brazier below the rim. There are vertical slits around the brazier, except at the junctions of the two sections, where the two apertures are crescent-shaped. Larger crescent-shaped apertures break up the surface of the base. On the mouthrim, three tooth-like projections at the centre and ends of the rounded section may have been intended to support a pot.

Glazed Pottery

154

151, 152, 153, 154, 155 & 156. **Dogs**
Eastern Han..........Green-glazed red earthenware
ht: 19.8 to 36.7 cm

As tomb guardians, the protective stance and fierce appearance exhibited by five of the six dogs on these two pages is quite appropriate: heads alert, legs squarely set, ready to defend. On the other hand, the animal in fig.154 looks rather like a pet dog begging for a morsel from its master.
All dogs have been formed by two-part moulds and added details modelled, some rather whimsically such as the incised eyebrows and whiskers of the dog in fig.152. The snarling expression of the animals in fig.151, 155 and 156 is a tribute to the potter's modelling skills.
A feature common to all dogs is their double harness: one collar circles the neck and the other the body, with the two collars joined at the nape of the neck by a large metal ring.
The glaze on fig.152 and 153 falls short of the legs while the animals in fig.151, 155 and 156 are totally glazed except for the underfeet. Fig.156 shows some iridescence. The sitting dog in fig.154 is remarkable in that the green glaze covering all but its stomach has become uniformly iridescent.

151

156

Glazed Pottery

152

155

157. Ram
Eastern Han..........Reddish earthenware with a green glaze
ht: 10.5 cm, length: 12 cm

The figure has emerged from a bivalve mould, with the seam left visible. The moulded decoration includes curled horns, a slightly open mouth and a bushy beard. There is also a short and stubby tail. The ram is short of his rear right leg, cut off just below the thigh. However, the cut edge is glazed, perhaps as a result of the glaze running during firing.

153

157

Glazed Pottery

159

159. Cockerel

Eastern Han..........*Red earthenware with an iridescent pale-green glaze*
ht: 11.5 cm

The prominent comb, the wing and tail feathers as well as the beak and eyes are moulded.
The mould includes a relatively high base on which stands the cockerel. The glaze on the underside of the base was wiped off prior to firing.

158. Duck ➤

Eastern Han..........*Red earthenware with an iridescent green glaze*
ht: 24 cm, length: 20.5 cm

This duck shows considerable care in its moulding and decoration. Parallel lines are incised on its head and down to its flat bill. Part of the wing plumage is depicted with circular punch marks which continue onto the breast; the rear part of the wings is incised with parallel horizontal lines. The back has two parallel lines which run across it, and the tail is also incised. A single row of punch marks between two parallel lines decorate the neck.
The duck is standing on broad webbed feet. The body is hollow.

Glazed Pottery

160

160. **Horse**
Eastern Han.........Red earthenware with an iridescent green glaze
ht: 31 cm, length: 36.5 cm

Perhaps representative of a pony, this short-legged animal stands firmly on all fours. Its open mouth suggests neighing.
Harness details have been moulded while a horse blanket has been incised over a solid cylindrical body.

164. **Hu** →
Eastern Han..........Red earthenware with a highly iridescent green glaze
ht: 48 cm, dia: 25 cm, dia (mouth): 15 cm

*Two **taotie** masks with nose rings are moulded on the shoulders. Double grooves decorate the mid-section and the junction between shoulder and neck. There are further grooves two-thirds of the distance between the body and rim, and on the flaring collar. Parallel striations appear below the groove. The unglazed base has lines indicating it was cut from the wheel with a cord.*
The glaze tends to flake off the body.

Glazed Pottery

161

161. Hu
Eastern Han..........Buff earthenware with a green, iridescent glaze
ht: 40.5 cm, dia: 32 cm, dia (mouth): 16 cm

The glaze is green with darker streaks stretching evenly down the vessel. The glaze has pooled and formed droplets on the flat top of the mouthrim, which bears three spur marks. The interior of the vessel is glazed from the mouthrim halfway down the neck.
The buff body was fired highly enough to give a resonant ring when struck.
A broad carved ring decorates the outside of the mouthrim. Two moulded **taotie** masks with rings were affixed to the vessel, centred upon a groove carved around the body's mid-section. Parts of the **taotie** masks have raised "seed" decoration imitating similar patterns on bronze objects.

162. Hu
Eastern Han..........Red earthenware with a streaky green glaze
ht: 42.6 cm, dia: 37 cm, dia (mouth): 19.2 cm

The clear green glaze has no iridescence, but some evenly-spaced streaks appear. Three spur marks are found on the rim.
Two moulded **taotie** masks with rings are applied to the body. Incised lines appear on the shoulder, with a band of triple zigzags perhaps applied by rouletting. Below the neck are three broad grooves with triangular design beneath the lowest groove. Other zigzag lines appear on the lower and upper parts of the neck.
The foot is flat, with some sand encrustations and cord-cut lines.

162

Glazed Pottery

166. **Hu**
Eastern Han.........*Green-glaze reddish earthenware*
ht: 37 cm

*The green glaze turns slightly amber as it approaches the foot. The interior is bare of glaze. On the shoulder two **taotie** masks with rings in their jaws glower. Deeply incised grooves score the lower rim, neck, shoulders, and mid-section. There are spur marks at the base.*

166

163

163. **Hu**
Eastern Han.........*Red earthenware with a highly iridescent green glaze*
ht: 32 cm, dia: 26.5 cm, dia (mouth): 12.3 cm

The body bears three evenly-spaced spur marks beneath the midpoint.
*A moulded frieze bears two **taotie** masks, and a hunting scene with two riders on horses, birds, rabbits, felines, rudimentary mountain motifs and a deer. Above the frieze are two raised circles, then two horizontal bands of rouletted design consisting of rectangular depressions below and a triple-line wave pattern above. The same pattern is repeated at the narrowest point of the neck, and then twice more on the exterior of the collared rim.*

Glazed Pottery

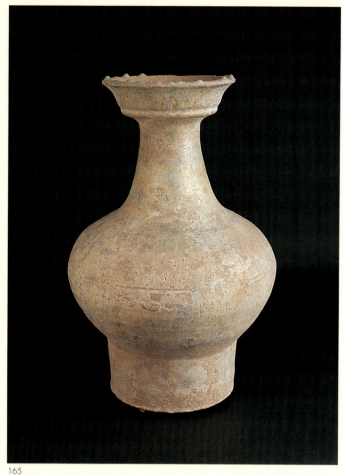

165.

165. *Hu*
Eastern Han..........Red earthenware with an iridescent green glaze
ht: 38 cm, dia: 25.5 cm, dia (mouth): 13.1 cm, dia (foot): 16 cm

The colour of the glaze varies from yellowish to mint to dark green, and has turned iridescent with tints of gold in places.
Decoration includes a zigzag band on the upper neck. On the shoulder from upper to lower portion, decoration consists of a groove, then a rouletted zigzag band, beneath which appears a faint zigzag motif. The base is flat and unglazed except for some probably accidental splashes. Signs of cord-cutting appear, and wedge-shaped spur marks. The foot is cylindrical and rather high (6.8 cm.).

167. *Hu*
Eastern Han..........Dark-orange earthenware with a highly iridescent green glaze
ht: 34.7 cm, dia (mouth): 13.6 cm

The glaze extends halfway down the interior of the neck. There are three rectangular spur marks on the base, which is completely glazed, and four spur marks on the rim.
*Two finely moulded **taotie** masks with rings on the shoulders are applied over two grooves. Other sets of grooves appear on the mouth rim, and on the upper shoulder.*

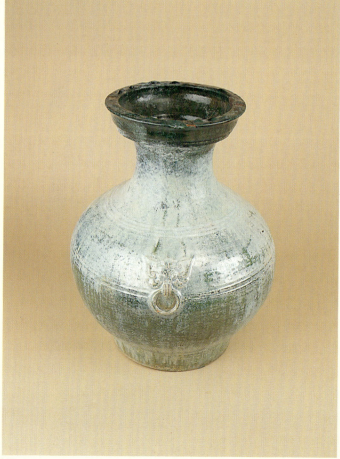

167.

Glazed Pottery

169. **Guan**
Eastern Han..........*Pinkish-orange earthenware with a dark-green glaze*
ht: 22.5 cm, dia (mouth): 12.3 cm

The glaze is clear and glossy, with fine crackles. Globular drops of glaze on the rim show that it was fired in an inverted position. Three spur marks appear on the rim and the base is glazed. Signs of wheel-throwing appear.

169

168

170

170. **Guan**
Eastern Han..........*Green-glazed reddish earthenware with iridescence*
ht: 12.5 cm, dia: 26 cm, dia (mouth): 9.5 cm

The glaze has formed thick droplets at the mouth, and has golden iridescent spots.
The body displays signs of wheel-throwing. The flat, glazed base bears three large rectangular spur marks.

168. **Guan**
Eastern Han..........*Green-glazed red earthenware with iridescence*
ht: 11 cm, dia: 14.5 cm, dia (mouth): 8 cm

The green glaze displays exceptional silvery iridescence. The interior is unglazed.
The body contains much mica. There are three spur marks on the lip. The glazed flat base rests on three wedge-shaped feet.

Glazed Pottery

174

174. Oil Lamp
Eastern Han..........Orange-red earthenware with a green glaze
ht: 27.5 cm, width: 11.3 cm

The lamp takes the form of a kneeling woman carrying two children in her arms. Above her head is a tall cylindrical extension like a tall headdress. The moulded lamp is hollow.

175. Oil Lamp
Eastern Han..........Green-glazed reddish earthenware with marked iridescence
ht: 26.5 cm, dia (cylinder): 6.5 cm

The hollow lamp has been moulded in the shape of a kneeling figure in a long robe, holding a child in her lap. The headgear is elongated upwards to form a cylinder.

175

Glazed Pottery

177. Oil Lamp
Eastern Han..........Pinkish-buff earthenware with an iridescent dark-green glaze
ht: 30 cm

The ceramic sculpture takes the form of a human figure on one knee, holding a child on its lap. The figure, which has a large nose, deep-set eyes and a cheeky expression, wears a belted robe. Both adult and child wear peaked hats. The adult figure is depicted holding the stem of a cylindrical lamp stand, undecorated except for grooves on the stem and the cupped oil holder.
The unglazed base shows the hollow body of the moulded lamp.

177

176

176. Oil Lamp
Eastern Han..........Red earthenware with an iridescent green glaze
ht: 22 cm

The lamp takes the form of a kneeling woman with a protruding belly, holding an infant to her breast; the top of her head continues upwards as a hollow cylinder.
The two sections of the lamp are joined down the sides to form a hollow body.

Glazed Pottery

171. Model of Brazier with Coal
Eastern Han..........Red earthenware with a highly iridescent green glaze
ht: 10.5 cm, dia: 12.5 cm

Two lug handles are affixed to the body beneath a flaring rim enclosing a top section of conical shape with perforations and diamond-shaped elements.

172. Jar with Lid
Eastern Han..........Green-glazed reddish earthenware
ht: 19 cm, dia: 18 cm

The jar is undecorated except for two incised lines around the shoulder. A salient feature of the vessel is the prominent channel into which the lid is fitted. The channel is most likely intended to hold water which would render the vessel air-tight, and also impede the entry of insects. This pragmatic construction is still seen in a traditional type of Chinese kitchen pot used for storing honey or pickles.
The concave base is glazed, with evidence of spur marks.

173. Seated Musician ➝
Eastern Han..........Reddish earthenware with an iridescent green glaze
ht: 15 cm

The kneeling musician wears a flat hat and a wrap-around robe. He tilts his head slightly to one side and closes his eyes in an attitude of concentration during his performance.
Mould seams are visible on the sides and top of the figure, which is hollowed to the midriff.

Glazed Pottery

178

178 & 179. Milling Sheds
Eastern Han..........Green-glazed red earthenware
178. ht: 22 cm, length: 21 cm
179. ht: 15.5 cm, length: 22.5 cm

Two figures are standing in front of a mill and a mortar and pestle grain pounder in fig. 178; the milling shed in fig. 179 also contains a mill, as well as a treadle-operated tilt hammer.
Both sheds have a gable roof with upturned eaves and finials at each end of the ridge. In fig. 178, the gable end walls stop short of the roof. In fig. 179, two square windows are cut into the back wall; the side walls extend out beyond the roof line to form low walls of curved profile on each side.
The interior of the sheds are only partially glazed. The glaze in fig. 178 is iridescent in places, especially on the roof.

179

183. Store-house →
Early to Mid Eastern Han..........Green-glazed red earthenware
ht: 38 cm, width: 31.5 cm, depth (roof): 27 cm

This unusual building model combines features of both the granaries and milling sheds.
A number of lines are scored across the front of the building to guide the laying out of decorative elements - a row of triangular, cut-out ventilation openings (which continue around the other three sides), two casement window-like shutters roughly sketched in, with a pole over fitting through three cleats. The last would seem to function as a device to secure the shutters.
The glaze is pale-green with darker green streaking and faint iridescence. The back is thinly glazed, while the interior and base are unglazed. There is a circular pontil mark on the unglazed base.

Glazed Pottery

180

180. Granary
Early to Mid Eastern Han..........*Green-glazed earthenware*
ht: 49.5 cm, width: 40.4 cm, depth: 21.5 cm

*This building type - with openings high up and lifted off the ground on feet - is generally recognised to be that of a granary. The model is of simple slab construction, with moulded elements added on. The overhanging gable roof has a central ridge with lateral rows of round tile covers which are capped at the eaves line with decorated tile ends. On the upper level, symmetrically placed openings with stamped lattice motifs on either side front on to a projecting balcony. The balcony has moulded railings and a central lattice-work panel, and is supported by **dougong** (or, traditional) brackets. There are marks suggesting that there may have been two figures on the balcony.*
The front feet are in the shape of bears while at the back they are simple slabs. The glaze, which has degraded to a pale-greenish colour, covers the front part of the roof, and the front and sides of the building only. It may be speculated that this manner of glazing indicates an axial or frontal placement of this object in the tomb.

182

182. Granary
Early to Mid Eastern Han..........*Green-glazed red earthenware*
ht: 55 cm, width: 45 cm

*This granary is similar to, but more elaborately decorated than fig.180 and fig.181. The roof, which has seven rows of tile covers instead of five, is itself supported by **dougong** brackets. A circular window has been cut between the two rectangular openings. Vertical balustrades divide the horizontal railings and lattice-work of the balcony, which is carried by small bear-shaped supports developed from projecting nibs. The front bear feet are well-moulded, with the characteristic prominent belly buttons and lively expressions.*
Some silvery iridescence is visible in spite of the extensive earth adhesions.

Glazed Pottery

181

181. Granary
Early to Mid Eastern Han..........Green-glazed reddish-pink earthenware
ht: 51.5 cm, length (roof): 43.5, depth (roof): 22.5 cm

*This granary is similar in design to fig. 180 except that the two windows are asymmetrically placed. There are also minor differences in the moulding of the bear feet, **dougong** brackets, and tile-ends.*
The mottled green glaze has some iridescence and is somewhat degraded.

Glazed Pottery

187. **Moated Tower** ➤
Eastern Han..........*Green-glazed red earthenware with some iridescence*
ht: 51 cm, dia (basin): 43 cm

The interior of the basin-like moat of this piece has an additional step, with the inner circle so formed possibly representing the water-line of the moat. A lively assortment of aquatic animals - ducks, fish, eel, and larger animals possibly geese - are found in the moat and on its banks. Dotted about the rim of the basin are more ducks, dogs, a frog, and possibly another goose.

*Rising above the moat is a square plan framed structure. Both the roof and the projecting balcony are supported by a complex structural system of cross struts and **dougong** bracketing. The brackets are not moulded as commonly found in other towers, but are here carefully made in three dimensions showing clearly how they tie back to the main framing members. The tiled roof has bird finials on the ridge as well as **akroteria** on the hip ridges.*

On the crowded balcony, two dancers are cavorting to the playing of four musicians on what appear to be wind and string instruments, and drums. This activity, and the open structure, suggests that this model may be the representation of some sort of pleasure pavilion. However, the presence of three cross-bowmen among the crowd does indicate that such buildings also served a defensive function.

A hole in the floor of the balcony, possibly representing a trap door, leads down to a mezzanine room created within the four corner posts of the tower.

The glaze has degraded to a whitish green, with areas of darker green.

Glazed Pottery

184. **Moated Watch-tower**
Mid to Late Eastern Han..........*Dark-green-glazed earthenware, with some iridescence*
ht: 64 cm, dia (basin): 36 cm

Composed of eight separate pieces stacked one on top of the other, this three-storey watch-tower sits in a deep basin representing a moat. Ducks, fish, and a chicken are disposed inside the moat (the chicken shows signs of being a later addition). More ducks are applied on the broad flat rim of the basin.
The bottom storey has either a door or a window cut into each side. Each opening has a projecting lintel. The two upper storeys are relatively lower in height, and have similar elements. Both have projecting balconies with cut-out railings. Human figures stand at each corner of the balconies. On both storeys, the square-sectioned room has slit windows with projecting lintels on all sides, similar to those of the bottom storey. The deeply overhanging hip roofs are glazed on both sides. For practical reasons of support, the roof of the middle storey develops into a square pedestal so that the storey above may sit securely on it.
Such towers give an indication of the elaborateness of later Han architecture, although the individual elements as modelled may be somewhat schematic and not always to scale.

Glazed Pottery

188. Moated Watch-tower
Mid to Late Eastern Han..........Green-glazed red earthenware
ht: 86 cm, dia (basin): 44.5 cm

*The stylised moat in which this four-storey watch-tower stands contains fish, tortoises, and a frog stuck to the bottom and sides. The first two storeys have the unusual feature of doorways cut into the front as well as rear walls, giving them an open and airy appearance. The balconies on the second and third storeys are respectively supported by bear-shaped pendants, and **dougong** brackets. The third storey is effectively a mezzanine, with low overhanging hip roof and cross bowmen at each corner bespeaking the defensive function of such towers. The slit windows with projecting lintels are similar to those in fig. 184. On the top, there are four more figures, gesturing with outstretched arms.*
The glaze has degraded to a light green tone, with areas of darker green, and has some silvery iridescence and earth adhesions.

Glazed Pottery

185. **Watch-tower**

Mid to Late Eastern Han.........*Green-glazed reddish earthenware, with iridescence*
ht: 118 cm, width (courtyard wall): 31 cm,
depth (courtyard wall): 24 cm

*The tower is composed of only four separate pieces, each somewhat smaller than the one below (cf. the eight pieces of fig. 184) and the tower stands in a compound of its own. An asymmetrically-placed entrance gateway with tiled roof gives on to a courtyard with a gable roof structure on the left. On the right, a ramp leads up to a side door of the first storey, which is raised above the level of the courtyard. A large pair of doors with **taotie** mask ring handles - perhaps the ceremonial entrance - remain firmly shut. On this level and the next one, the post-and-beam construction, with decorative bosses or round nail heads at the junctions, is clearly visible.*

*Each storey has projecting lattice windows just below the hipped roof. The lattices are now mostly filled in with earth, but it can be seen in a few places that they are actually pierced through in a faithful representation of their function as ventilators. The roofs themselves are supported by a combination of **dougong** brackets and diagonal roof-struts at the corners. The **dougong** brackets have a dragon head pendant. Large quatrefoil moulded florets are applied at the junction of strut and roof. On each of the upper storeys, a figure stands at the balcony parapet in front of the doorway. The second storey has more decorative detail than the other storeys.*

Like the granary models, the front facade of this tower tends to be more heavily loaded with decorative motifs. The rear of the tower is also largely unglazed, except for the top storey. All this suggests a frontal or axial placement of such building models in the tomb.

Much of the dark-green glaze has flaked off. However, there are areas of gold iridescence, especially on the side walls of the top two storeys.

Glazed Pottery

186. Watch-tower

Mid to Late Eastern Han..........Green-glazed reddish-buff earthenware
ht: 104 cm, width: 30 cm, depth: 38 cm

This watch-tower is similar in some respects to fig.184. The projecting, tray-like balconies are used as separate stacking elements. The first storey is proportionally much higher than the upper storeys, as in fig.184. In other respects, however, this tower resembles fig.185. The walled compound, projecting latticed windows above doorways, figures standing in doorways, details of post-and-beam construction, and roof-struts with moulded florets are all found here also.

Features unique to this tower include the standing figures on the balcony ledges, a moulded bear applique on the second storey parapet wall, and the dragon head gargoyles below. At courtyard level, two galloping horses, one with a rider, emerge from the gateway. The courtyard wall has a neatly made tiled coping.

The pale green glaze is degraded in places.

186

Glazed Pottery

189

*189. **Well-head***
Early Eastern Han.........Green-glazed red earthenware
ht: 21 cm, dia: 15 cm

There are three grooves carved around the middle of the well-head, at the top of the lower, straight-sided section. It may be speculated from the proportions that this lower section is meant to be below ground. Other examples of well-heads are known where this lower section is so exaggerated in height that there is no doubt that the underground portion is being represented.
There are two small holes of approximately 5mm in diameter on opposite sides of the ledge. Other well-heads are known where similar holes are found in a flange around the base. It may be speculated that such holes indicate where a frame or superstructure would have been erected over the well-head for the attachment of a pulley and ropes. The glaze is somewhat degraded.

Glazed Pottery

190. **Well-head (right)**
Eastern Han..........*Green-glazed pink earthenware*
ht: 25.5 cm, width (ledge): 13.5 cm

*Well-head with A-frame superstructure and pot resting on a **jing** shaped ledge. The glaze is of dark-green tone, with earth adhesions. The base is unglazed.*

190. **Well-head (left)**
Eastern Han..........*Green-glazed pinkish earthenware*
ht: 50 cm, width (ledge): 21.5 cm

This cylindrical well-head has a flat ledge composed of four straight members which intersect at the corners. The A-frame superstructure sports two dragon-head gargoyles, and a square-framed housing for a pulley which is topped with a tiled hip roof.
The container resting on the ledge of the well is studded, suggesting a non-ceramic material. It has two rounded flanges rising up from its sides which are pierced, which may indicate that this is a water bucket meant for lowering into the well with the help of a pulley and ropes.
The glaze has earth adhesions and traces of iridescence, especially on the water bucket. The base is unglazed.

190

193. **Well-head**
Eastern Han..........*Green-glazed pinkish-buff earthenware, with iridescence*
ht: 27.5 cm, dia: 15.4 cm

*This well-head is similar to fig. 192 except more heavily made. A groove is carved into the slightly bulging sides. A water pot with carinated body rests on the ledge. The pulley is visible, and the square frame of the pulley housing is moulded with a **jing** character (well) - an instance where this character is used in a purely decorative manner.*
The glaze has wine-coloured suffusions due to reduction clouding.

193

Glazed Pottery

191

191. **Well-head**
Eastern Han.........Green-glazed pinkish-buff earthenware
ht: 51.5 cm, width (ledge): 18.5 cm

This well is similar in size and design to the larger example in fig. 190 except that the well-head has inward sloping sides which results in the upright struts of the A-frame superstructure being pushed more closely together. The pulley - a wheel with a deeply grooved rim along which the rope passes - is clearly visible.
The glaze has extensive staining and degradation, but also some areas of yellowish-silvery iridescence. The base is cord-cut.

Glazed Pottery

192

192. **Well-head**
Eastern Han.........*Red earthenware with a highly iridescent dark-green glaze*
ht: 29.8 cm, dia: 19 cm

The sides of this well are marked out by three carved grooves - one around the waisted top section, and two around the straight-sided lower section which is further decorated with a freely combed band. The superstructure is arch-shaped and made in two sections, each incorporating part of the frame of the pulley housing. However no pulley or cross-member is shown. The roof on top of the pulley housing is a simple, two-way pitched roof, not a hip roof as on the examples with A-frame superstructures. The interior is glazed around the neck only.

Glazed Pottery

194

194. Sheep Pen
Eastern Han..........Red earthenware with an iridescent green glaze
ht (pen): 6 cm, ht (overall): 11.5 cm, dia: 21.5 cm

The pen, in the form of a circular, straight walled dish, contains four moulded rams with pointed faces and prominent, curved horns. A fifth much larger ram, with different features, carries a rider or shepherd. Seated on a saddle cloth, with one hand grasping his mount's horns, the rider has his head turned to one side.

197. Pigsty
Eastern Han..........Reddish earthenware with a dark-green glaze
ht: 12 cm, length: 18 cm, width: 17 cm, length of pigs: 11.5 cm

The enclosure wall, made with one slab of clay curled around a flat base, has a ramp and landing to one side. One of the pigs seems to have escaped and crouches on the landing looking down at its companion rooting in the sty.
The interior of the sty is only partially glazed.

197

Glazed Pottery

195

195. Double Animal Pen
Eastern Han.........Pinkish-buff earthenware with an iridescent dark-green glaze
ht: 18.3 cm, width: 27 cm, length: 40 cm

The entrances lead into two separate enclosures, each containing animals and farmyard structures, and each roughly daubed with glaze. On the right-hand side, four goats emerge from a shed, adjacent to a two-storey structure. A human figure is seated clasping his knees, on the ramp or ladder in front of this structure. The left-hand enclosure has a lean-to which shelters two pigs in a sty, and a large, bird-like animal in front of a hipped-roof shed.
There is a wedge-shaped kiln support and the mark of another, of similar size, on the base.

198

198. Pigsty and Shed
Eastern Han.........Red earthenware with an iridescent dark-green glaze
ht: 8 cm, length: 19 cm, depth: 14.5 cm

This square sty is formed by four slab walls, one with a curved notch cut out of it. Within, a sow suckles five piglets, and another animal possibly also a pig, is drinking or feeding from a trough. Outside the sty is a small tiled-roof shed.

Glazed Pottery

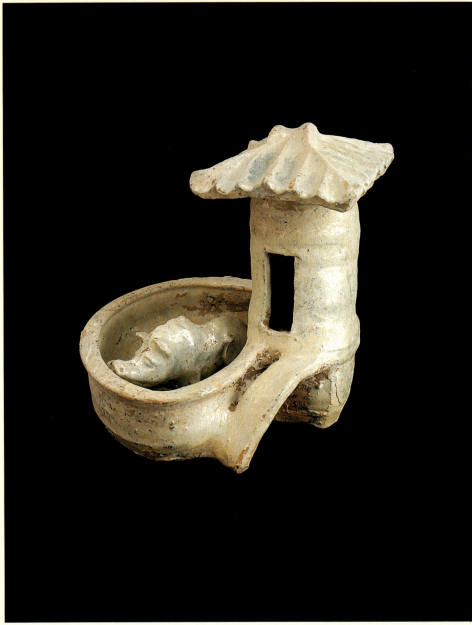

199

199. Pigsty and Privy
Eastern Han.........Red earthenware with a fully iridescent green glaze
ht: 21.5 cm, dia: 22 cm

A clearly moulded pig with bristly mane and prominent snout stands within the semi-circular, dish-like sty. On one side, outside the sty, a ramp leads up to a privy with hipped tile roof. The floor of the privy is cut out so that it connects through to the sty - a graphic early illustration of the recycling of human waste.
The interior of the privy and the base are unglazed.

Glazed Pottery

196. **Animal Pen**
Eastern Han.........*Green-glazed pinkish-buff earthenware*
ht: 14.5 cm, length: 21.5 cm, width: 20.5 cm

A symmetrically positioned gateway with tiled roof and door ajar leads into a yard crowded with animals - three goats, a ram, and two sheep. At the back, there is a lean-to, providing shelter for the animals. This space extends below an adjacent raised upper portion with slot-shaped opening, which is possibly a dwelling.
The unusual feature of this animal pen is the animals which have been left unglazed, or in the biscuit. They have been placed in position after the application of the glaze, and contrast strongly with the green glaze covering the rest of the piece, which has acquired an even, whitish green iridescence.

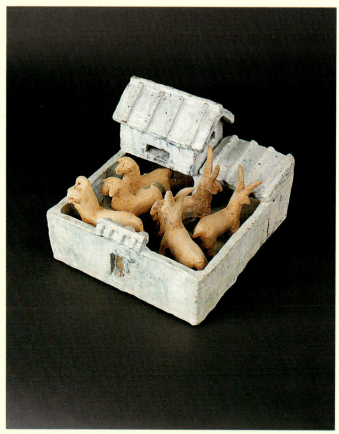

196

200

200. **Pigsty and Privy**
Eastern Han.........*Green-glazed earthenware*
ht: 15 cm, length: 25 cm, width: 25 cm

This rectangular sty has raised wall sections at the corners. Within, two standing pigs face a trough and one is lying on its side. Next to the sty, a stepped ramp with handrail on one side leads up to a privy of substantial size. The privy has scored lattice panels on either side of the entrance, and a tiled gable roof with ridge finials.
The glossy glaze is of clear green tone and is slightly mottled, with some slight iridescence.

Glazed Pottery

Proto-Greenware

202

202. **Globular Jar**
Western Han..........*Pinkish-buff body with a mottled olive glaze*
ht: 30 cm, dia: 34 cm, dia (mouth): 8 cm

The unglazed lower half of the jar is burnt reddish brown. The upper body bears two moulded handles surmounted with a stylized animal head motif and topped with a clay scroll. The lower parts of the handles have combed incised lines. The base is slightly concave.

204. **Jar**
Western Han..........*Buff body with a watery green glaze*
ht: 24.8 cm, dia: 26 cm, dia (mouth): 8.4 cm

The upper body is incised with three sets of three grooves. The loop handles with appliqued spirals and distinct miniature human figures are affixed to the shoulder. The base is slightly concave.

203

204

203. **Jar**
Western Han..........*Pale-buff body with a mottled olive-yellow glaze*
ht: 23.1 cm, dia: 24.5 cm, dia (mouth): 8.2 cm

Decoration is confined to a set of triple incised lines on the neck, two more sets on the upper body, and one on the lower unglazed portion. Two handles exist, with a scrolled clay motif above. The base is flat with a slightly depressed ring possibly caused by a kiln support.

205. **Ovoid Jar**
Western Han..........*Reddish body with a light-olive glaze*
ht: 32.5 cm, dia: 39 cm, dia (mouth): 11.6 cm

The lower half of the body is undecorated. The upper half bears three raised strips with square cross-section. Above the mid-line are lightly inscised birds. There are two **taotie** *masks with handles.*

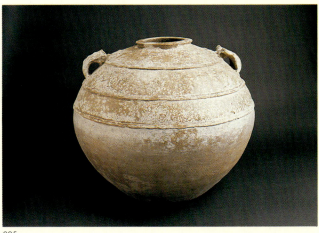

205

201.

201. *Jar with Mask-handles*
Western Han..........Buff-coloured body with an olive-green glaze
ht: 15 cm, dia: 22 cm, dia (mouth): 7 cm

Striking double mask-handles give character to this squat globular jar. The jar has a low flattened mouth rim. Three incised lines enclosing two bands of combed wavy decoration circle the jar at the level of the mask-handles.
The streaky glaze covers the top half of this high-fired vessel and part of the interior. Three short rectangular feet are attached to the flat, cord-cut base.

Proto-Greenware

207. Pair of Jars
Late Western Han..........Buff body with a clear glaze
ht: 17 cm, dia: 14 cm, dia (mouth): 8.5 cm

The vessels are decorated with a band of wavy combed motifs around the base of the neck. At the shoulder are plain loop handles. Corresponding to the positions of the upper and lower ends of the loop handles are double incised lines circling the jars. Evenly spaced rounded ridges provide a visual rhythm on the unglazed lower part of the jars.
Both jars have a shallow footrim.

207

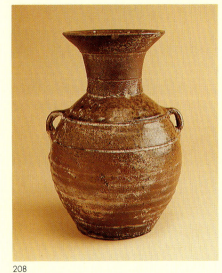
208

208. Hu
Late Western Han..........Dark-brown body with an olive-green glaze
ht: 20 cm, dia: 14 cm, dia (mouth): 10 cm

The glaze stops just beneath the handles, and extends into the interior of the flared mouth.
The neck is decorated with an incised wavy band. Two small neatly-made handles are decorated with criss-cross incisions.

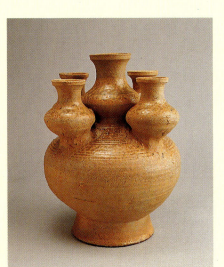
209

209. Quintuple Hu
Late Eastern Han..........Buff body with a yellowish-green glaze
ht: 26 cm, dia: 20 cm

Flaking glaze covers the upper portion.
The central **hu** bears two incised horizontal lines on its shoulder. The lower body is incised with two more sets of three incised lines.

Proto-Greenware

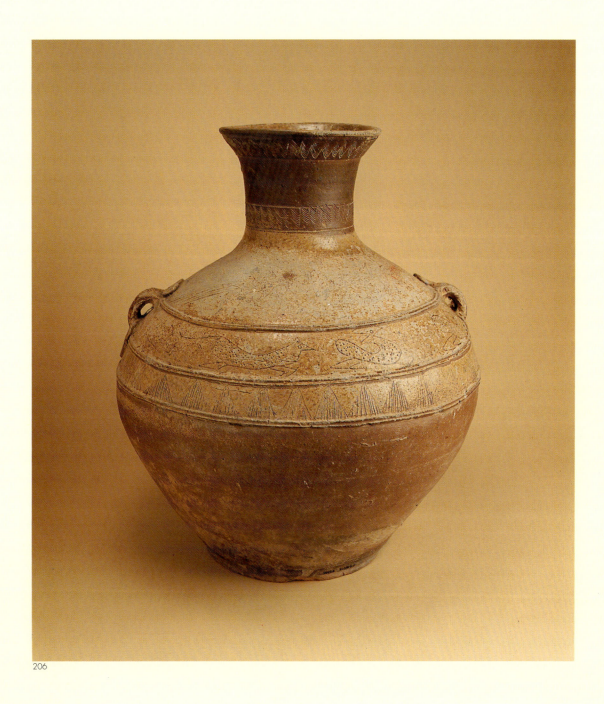

206.

206. **Hu**
Western Han..........*Grey-coloured body with a greenish-yellow glaze*
ht: 41 cm, dia: 34 cm

Glaze appears on both exterior and interior, but extends only from the mid-line to the neck. The exposed part of the stoneware body has been burnt aubergine.
The neck possesses combed decor at top and bottom, enclosed by incised parallel lines. Beneath the glaze is an incised decoration divided into three horizontal panels, separated by double raised lines. The top panel consists of five motifs possibly depicting birds. The middle panel contains six figures of quadrupeds. The lower panel is decorated with incised triangles. Two vertical handles are incised in a pattern resembling woven basketry with a ring below, and double spiral above.

Proto-Greenware

True Greenware

212.

212. **Hu**
Late Eastern Han..........*Red body with a black glaze*
ht: 13.5 cm, dia: 10.5 cm

The glaze is dark-green to black. The body is dark-red, burnt grey where exposed during firing.
Decoration is confined to moulded concentric lines around the top of the base, the mid-section, and the bottom of the neck, and a deep groove beneath the upper lip. The base is slightly concave, unglazed.

210. **Hu** →
Late Eastern Han or later..........*Buff body with a light-olive glaze*
ht: 24 cm, dia: 24 cm

The glaze, which stops short of the foot, contains many dark iron spots. Decoration is limited to two single horizontal handles, and two sets of two vertical handles set on parallel horizontal lines incised under the glaze.

211. ***House*** →
Late Eastern Han or later..........*Grey body with a greyish-green glaze*
ht: 18.5 cm, width: 13.5 cm, depth: 12.5 cm

The roof of this small house is unlike those of the other building models in this book. It is not a flat slab, but curves in two directions, with a shallow sag characteristic of many Chinese roofs known from later examples. There are tile wind-breaks set well back from the gable end, over alternating rows of concave and convex pantiles between. The ridge, upturned at both ends, is decorated with an incised cross-hatch pattern, a wavy strip of clay along the top, and a gourd-shaped finial in the middle.
A doorway and two square windows are cut out at the front of the house, with further windows in the side walls.
The opaque, crackled glaze covers the exterior of the building. The interior and base are unglazed.

True Greenware

List of Lenders

Marjorie Chu	161
Empress Place Collection	11, 53, 183
Mr & Mrs Borge Forssell	35, 48, 49, 191, 203
Mr & Mrs Roberto Galeotti	147
Mrs Kristina Gardin	98
Mr & Mrs Johnny K G Goh	163, 192, 205
Mrs Juliana Goh	71
Mr K T Goh	18, 23, 25, 26, 47, 92, 93, 95, 109, 119, 127, 134
Dr K Kwok	77, 78, 79
Aileen Lau	199
Lee Kong Chian Art Museum, National University of Singapore	5, 12, 29, 74, 105, 133, 188, 194, 206, 209
Purchase: Lee Foundation Fund	1, 4, 14, 31, 69, 73, 75, 86, 88, 117, 144, 152, 178, 182, 197, 210, 211
Purchase: Shaw Foundation Grant	69, 106, 176
Dr & Mrs Lim Kuang Hui	165
Mr & Mrs T S Loh	13, 36, 162
Dr & Mrs Earl Lu	30, 103, 110, 118, 123, 153, 202, 204
Mr & Mrs Amir Mallal	54, 83, 114, 125, 154, 158, 181
National Museum, Singapore	33, 76, 80, 136, 179
Purchase: Shaw Foundation Grant	8, 9, 21, 22, 24, 43, 51, 55, 58, 59, 65, 68, 91, 121, 145, 149, 160, 175, 186, 187
Dr & Mrs Ivan Polunin	126
Raffles Country Club Art Museum	2, 20, 42, 108, 113, 122, 164
Mr & Mrs Ronald Shen	102, 104, 115, 138, 151, 167, 169, 195, 196, 200
Lucina Talib Collection	126, 129
Mr Tan Hui Seng	34, 97, 130, 174, 198
Mrs Annie Wee	17, 39, 45, 56, 57, 60, 61, 67, 84, 120, 139, 141, 142, 143, 148, 155, 157, 159, 173, 177, 180, 184
Mr & Mrs H C Wong	124, 140, 150
Mr & Mrs S T Yeo	3, 15, 16, 27, 37, 40, 46, 62, 63, 64, 85, 87, 90, 100, 107, 112, 166, 172, 201, 207
Mr & Mrs Frank Yip Mien Chun	6, 19, 28, 50, 94, 111, 116, 128, 131, 132, 135, 137, 146, 168, 171, 189, 190
Private Collection	7, 10, 41, 70, 72, 81, 193
Private Collection	32, 44, 82, 156, 185,
Private Collection	38, 66
Private Collection	96, 99, 101, 212
Private Collection	170
Private Collection	208

GLOSSARY

ASH GLAZE A high-fired glaze in which ash (usually derived from wood or other vegetal matter) acts as a flux. The presence of ash also introduces colouring and the yellowish-green colour of the Han high-fired wares is due to the natural presence in the glaze of iron and titanium oxides.

BISCUIT Fired but unglazed clay body.

BLACKWARE A high-fired ware of the greenware family, whose coarse and dark body is covered with an almost black glaze; the dark colour is due to the relatively high iron content, 4–5%, as compared to the lighter greenware which contains 1–2%.

BOSHAN LU (博山炉) The ancient goblet form was re-fashioned in the Han period as a censer for burning aromatics imported from Southeast Asia. New features were a conical top with perforations to release the smoke, and a dish at the foot of the vessel to catch burning ash particles. The mountain peaks moulded on the top or cover represented the Daoist paradise of the Immortals.

CI (瓷) A high-fired (around 1300 degrees C), waterproof clay body which contains kaolin and produces a ringing sound when tapped; it is usually coated with a high-fired felspathic glaze. In the English language, this material is called stoneware, or, when the impurities are totally removed from the clay so that it is white and translucent, it is called porcelain.

CORD-CUT Refers to the manner in which a thrown pot is separated from the wheel by sliding a cord between the pot and the wheel; the cord leaves an unmistakable mark which is commonly found on the bases of Han wares of regular shape.

DING (鼎) A three-legged cauldron used for cooking in neolithic times. The "ding" served as a ritual bronze in the Shang and Zhou dynasties, but functioned in the Han largely as a cooking pot. Its popularity apparently waned after the introduction of the kitchen range which could hold more than one vessel.

DOUGONG (斗拱) A system of brackets inserted between the top of a column and a cross-beam, each bracket being formed by a double bow-shaped arm called "gong" and a block of wood called "dou" on each side.

ERBEI (耳杯) Oval wine cup with horizontal flanges which suggest ears or wings. The form and decorative motifs of pottery "erbei" follow those of lacquer models.

GREY POTTERY Pottery which has undergone reduction firing, whereby the iron in the clay has deoxidized, turning the fired clay to grey. Grey wares go back to neolithic times. However, improved firing techniques during the Han dynasty resulted in a hard, uniformly coloured ware whose quality was not surpassed in subsequent periods.

GUAN (罐) A bottle-like jar with a constricted neck.

HU (壶) The variant pottery forms derive from a ritual bronze wine vessel prototype. Generally, the "hu" has a broad low-slung body, sloping shoulders and a narrow neck flaring out at the mouth. It usually has ring handles and may have a cover.

IRIDESCENCE Refers to the silvery, or more rarely golden, lustre-like surface which lead-glazed wares acquire after prolonged exposure to heavy moisture. Once it has begun, this corrosion is an ongoing process, and layers form successively, one on top of the other. The Chinese refer to this phenomenon as silvery frost. In addition to being found on the green lead glazes of the Han, iridescence has also been observed on the green lead-glazed wares of later periods. The technical term for the process by which glass or glaze degrades, and sometimes produces this effect, is known as devitrification.

LEAD GLAZES Decorative glazes associated especially with the Han and Tang dynasties. In a lead glaze, lead oxide makes up at least 50% of the glaze and acts as a flux. Since this flux works effectively within a wide range of low to medium temperatures (from 500 degrees C to 1100 degrees C), lead glazes lend themselves well to use with earthenware. The addition of iron oxide produces an amber to brown colour whereas the addition of copper oxide produces a dark green colour, the latter by far the most favoured during Eastern Han.

LIAN (奩) A straight-sided cylindrical vessel. Some flat-topped "lian" in lacquer and bronze were used to hold cosmetics. Some pottery "lian" found in Han tombs often had domed lids and are also described as hill jars.

GLOSSARY

MINGQI (明器) Objects designed specifically for use in tombs. Most Han "mingqi" consisted of copies of bronze or lacquer vessels, or models of architectural forms, figures and animals made of earthenware.

PIGMENT From the Western Zhou period (1066-770 BC) to the Three Kingdoms (220-65), grey pottery was sometimes decorated with unfired pigments applied with a brush. These mineral-based pigments imitated inlay work on bronzes, painting on lacquerware, or simply added definition to certain features of the wares. The Han palette included red, green, purple, blue, brown, yellow, black and white. Because the pigments were unfired, they wore off or faded and many pieces only hint at what their original appearance must have been like.

POTTERY A generic term used to describe objects which are made of clay. In a broad sense, the word pottery refers to earthenware, stoneware and porcelain. However, in ceramic terms, pottery refers to low-fired wares, that is wares usually fired at temperatures ranging between 700 degrees C and 1100 degrees C. In this case, the word pottery is interchangeable with earthenware.

PROTO-GREENWARE The forerunner of true greenware, proto-greenware is a high-fired ware with a yellowish to green glaze. However, it does not contain all of the ingredients and properties ascribed to "ci". The first proto-greenware, no doubt produced accidentally when wood ash fluxed the surface of the ware in the course of firing, goes as far back as the Shang dynasty.

RELIEF MOULDING A decorative technique also known as sprigging whereby small clay elements are applied directly to the main body to create a relief form. Sprigs may be freely modelled after they have been applied to the pot or they may have been previously pressed in a mould. Relief moulding on large surfaces, such as the walls of hill-jars, is the result of the entire piece having been formed in a mould of which the relief decoration is part.

TAO (陶) A low-fired, porous clay body; in the English language, it is referred to as pottery or earthenware.

TAOTIE (饕餮) The motif is composed of a pair of confronting zoomorphs seen in profile which also form an animal mask seen in full face. Depicted on bronze and pottery vessels, the motif refers to a devouring monster that is itself eaten, and is therefore considered to be a warning against greed..

TRUE GREENWARE A high-fired ware which, in addition to having all the characteristics of "ci", has a greenish-coloured glaze. The colour is due to the fact that the glaze contains iron and that the ware has been fired in a reduction atmosphere.

XUAN WEN (弦纹) Bowstring motif; relief lines or narrow ridges such as those found on Han "hu" and granary jars.

YI (匜) A low bowl-like ewer which may have feet or a flat base. Generally used to hold water.

ZUN (樽) A generic name for a ritual wine vessel with both wooden and metal prototypes.

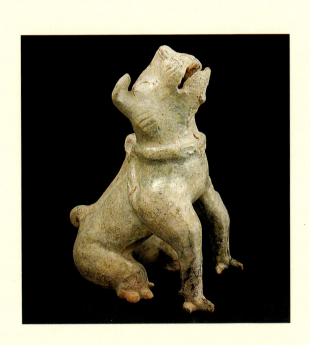